Playing Above The Line

Brett Odgers

First Published in 2015
By Odd-Guy Pty Ltd

Sydney, Australia

Online coaching program is available at
www.playingabovetheline.com/online-coach

Odgers Brett
Playing above the line: Creating a winning team.
ISBN: 978-0-9943007-0-6

Cover Design by Brett Odgers
Layout by Brett Odgers
Edited by Naomi Csoke

CHAMPION TEAMS

"Greatness doesn't happen by chance, nor does it occur in a vacuum. Greatness comes from, first, a passion for what you do; and second, a clear understanding of what you can and want to be best at." - Blair Singer

What business leaders have to say about Playing Above the Line and working with Brett Odgers

Playing Above the Line provides fantastic coaching for you and for your team!

Marshall Goldsmith
World famous executive coach and author of the New York Times bestsellers, Triggers and What Got You Here Won't Get You There.

This book is a great reminder of how to bring the best out in your self and others. It is a practical and insightful read that should be on the essential reading list for the everyone

Deidre Anderson
Elites sport transition specialist
Deputy vice chancellor
Macquarie University.

Brett has the ability to influence young people in a language they understand.

Many people have written books about team work. But very few have lived the experience as Brett did.

Stan Jordan
Promoter and Entrepreneur

Playing Above the Line is an indispensable read for anyone leading or participating in a team. The principles are readily transferable to any team, be that work, sport, community or home.

His storytelling power is evident as he draws you into the journey of his teenage soccer team on their quest to be the best – CHAMPIONS! It is a simple yet " spot on " message that inspires energises and creates hope for how a team should be.

I could easily relate to the challenges of Brett as the coach, particularly in regards to individuals within a team finding excuses, blaming others and not holding themselves accountable. Negative behaviours that we all allow ourselves to slip into, ultimately undermining the individual and team.

This book is very relevant to today's young generation. Instead of the ME generation it inspires us to be the WE generation and become effective thriving teams in life.

Brett writes with an authenticity that resonates with the average person as well as the corporate high flyer, empowering and encouraging us all to be a collective of extraordinary people!

Tracy Tallentire – Business owner

This book really is a road map on how to build a winning team. While it's a story about a teenage soccer team it is highly relevant to anyone working in a team. Especially in business.

I can recognise some of the characters Brett has to deal with in his soccer team, they are almost the same as people I know at work.

The story was written in an easy to read conversational style.

Clive Jones – Business Leader

Need more help?

The Audiobook is available via our website
www.PlayingAboveTheLine.com

A self-guided Online Coaching Program is also available
www.PlayingAboveTheLine.com/online-coach

The Daily Disciplines App is coming soon
To help you stay above the line

Brett is available for speaking engagements & workshops
Please contact us
business@playingabovetheline.com

PLAYING ABOVE THE LINE

CONTENTS

Introduction

This book is a story of a group of young people who started from behind the eight ball and became a winning team. They chose to work at becoming a champion team. Not a team of individual champions all looking for attention and glory for themselves

They achieved a level of performance that even shocked themselves. And this is their story......

...but it's a parable for our lives and our work.

This group took total responsibility for their individual contribution...

......and eliminated blame, excuses and drama from their work.

In other words.....They learned to play above the line

And they had the turnaround in performance of their lives.

For many people the only memories of playing team sports are rough, tough and mean.

This year I wanted much more than that for my team of 15 year olds. I wanted the experience of playing Soccer in this team to be as valuable as it was memorable. I wanted these young people to have a real experience of what it's like to work in an amazing team.

To work in a team where they could be the best they were capable of personally and together. I wanted to teach them much more than just Soccer. I wanted to teach them what they could achieve when they chose greatness. And I wanted them to carry these lessons through what will be the most challenging years of their lives.

Instead of teaching them more Soccer skills, I taught them teamwork and personal responsibility. And the result was extraordinary.

Leadership style

Inspiring

Coaching

Entrusting

Supportive

Instructive

Directive

controlling

Team Model

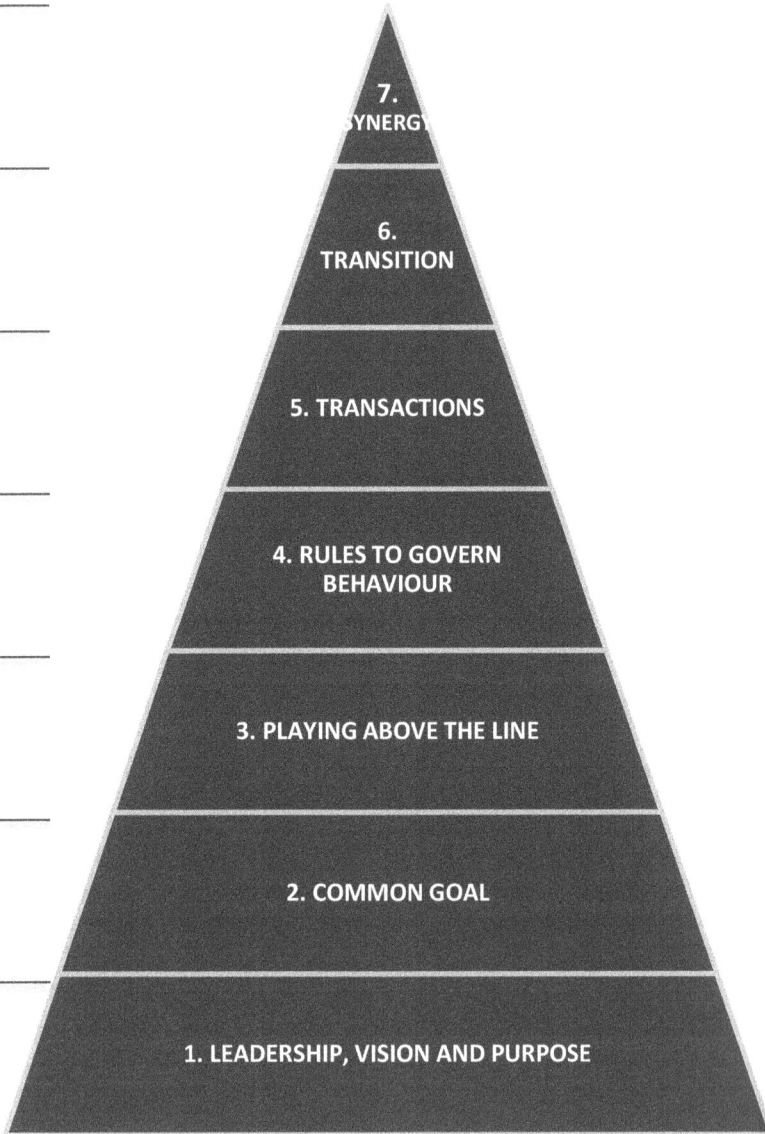

7. SYNERGY

6. TRANSITION

5. TRANSACTIONS

4. RULES TO GOVERN BEHAVIOUR

3. PLAYING ABOVE THE LINE

2. COMMON GOAL

1. LEADERSHIP, VISION AND PURPOSE

ACKNOWLEDGMENTS

I want to thank those who believed that doing something different, bold and audacious had potential for great results, and those who allowed me to coach them, to lead them on a journey we'll never forget.

CHAPTER 1.
A BOLD EXPERIMENT

I've seen it in families that faced the fire of challenges and pulled through. I've seen sports teams and businesses that have come together as a team, faced unimaginable pressure, overcoming huge obstacles, and come out the other side; closer, stronger and victorious.

I was now coaching a group of teenage soccer players.
I wanted them to not only have a great football season, but to experience working in a team in a way that might help them through the turbulent teenage years ahead. I wanted to make an impression on them and help them grow up to be amazing young men and women.

But right now, I was sitting in a conference room in the city with about 60 other Business Coaches learning the intricacies of Behavioural Coaching.

My mind, however, was elsewhere. I was sitting in this classroom while my team were on a soccer field facing what was their biggest challenge for the season so far. Whatever we were meant to be learning for the next 45 minutes was lost to me.

Playing above the line

The game they were in the midst of was a big test for them. The group of teenagers that I'd been coaching for the past few years were facing one of their biggest rivals and I wasn't there with them. Not in the physical form anyway.

As I sat in the lecture I kept thinking *'could this group of soccer players come together as a team and stay strong or would they fall apart without a coach there?'*

The Team
My ragtag group of soccer players were facing a game against last years champions, who had a psychological advantage over us having won 5 of the last 8 encounters.

We were about half way through our season and things had turned around remarkably.

Last year the team had lots of enthusiasm, with some players proving to have exceptional skill, but they still finished in the bottom half of the group. They would fall to pieces when the pressure got too much. Players would start yelling at each other, blaming their team mates, and excuses would creep into our game. Eventually, players would end up remonstrating to the ref as their opposition streaked past them to finish us off. After the game, their pubescent tempers would take flight and it would turn ugly.

This was not why I wanted to coach young people in soccer. I believe that games are a reflection of life and that the skills you bring to the field of sport will be reflected in other areas of your own life. I wanted these wonderful young guys to learn much more than just soccer.

This season however was a different matter, a whole new beast. We had the same team as last year but so far we were undefeated. But today, we faced a huge test; our arch rivals who had spanked us several times previously, were back. What's more is they didn't even have their own coach or assistant coach. They just had themselves to rely on to hold it all together.

As in any group of teenagers, we had a few who were quite full of themselves and knew without hesitation that their way was the best way, despite evidence to the contrary. Would these guys take over and destroy the strong sense of what it means to be a winning team, something that we had been working on over the past few months?

Would the spectators and well meaning parents take over and make "helpful suggestions" about how we needed to play?

I couldn't know any of that because I was stuck in a classroom, connected only by text messages surreptitiously read while the lecturer talked.

I had prepared them at training through the week and given everyone their assignments and positions, but more importantly, I had prepared them for what to do if we went behind and it started to fall to pieces.

The easiest way I could think to convey this was with 2 rules that I drilled into them.

The first...

1. No Blame & No Excuses.

Basically NO JUSTIFICATION.

No matter what happens, assume everyone who is on the field is giving their best, so no blame. If you are tempted to trash talk anyone, don't! Not to your team mates, not to the opposition and not to the ref.

And if you aren't giving your best, theres no excuse. Find a solution and find it quick. If you are out of position, get back in it. If you lose the ball, retrieve it. If you are tired, get off and rest. If your team mate doesn't have an option, give him one.

The second saying, and this is one of my favourites...

2. Never, ever, ever, give up.

This game was a big challenge and they were doing it without supervision. Would they fall to pieces? Descend into a fairly typical cycle of individuals playing wherever they wanted? Would strong personalities take over and if they went down a goal or 2, could they pick themselves back up?

I anxiously awaited news as I sat in the class room. About half way through the first half we scored. 1:0. My heart soared, but I knew the opposition would hit back hard, they had some great strikers with brilliant pace.

Just before the half time break they did just that leveling the score with a goal. 1:1 at half time.

At half time, the team knew what they had to do. They grouped together and our captain asked the team 2 questions;

> 1. What are we doing best?
> 2. And what could we be doing better?

I'm fairly certain a few of the parents would have put in their 2 cents worth but it probably didn't even register. When your captain asks you what you could be doing better it starts a conversation in your head that leads to changes you choose to make. I've seen it time and again. They would have discussed a few ideas amongst themselves and reorganised themselves ready for the 2nd half of the game.

In past games, the opposing team had come back and slaughtered us from just such a position. I was anxious that they kicked off the 2nds half string but the opposition coach is a mate of mine and a good coach, so he would be advising his team to do the same.

I texted… *Any News?*
No reply.

Again… *What's happening?*

Still nothing.

I was fearing the worst at this point when my phone buzzed. I glanced at it to see a text from my wife.

Sorry, game is thrilling couldn't tear myself away.
We just scored another!

I was slightly relieved. This put us in front by one, making the score 2:1 with about 15 minutes left to play. It's a dangerous score line because you don't know whether to defend the lead or continue to attack. My philosophy has always been to defend by attacking. Nothing is more exciting for a team than to press the advantage and either win with style or lose with heroic dignity having given it your all.

Whatever was being taught in that classroom for the next 15 minutes fell on deaf ears because I was lost in thought as to what might be happening to the team.

Are they descending into blame and excuses as I saw happen so many times last year or are they synced into one another, communicating as if by magic?

A few minutes later I had my answer, the final whistle blew with us winning 3:1. You beauty! What a legendary team, with an amazing bunch of young people.

This not only put us in the lead for the championship but it meant we were undefeated and we were most of the way through the season.

They had played as a team that was bound together with an unusual code of honour. It was the way they thought about teams and football that separated them from the opposition that day.

I caught up with my mate, the opposition coach, and he said to me. *"At the end of the game I debriefed my guys and asked them what they thought was the difference between the two teams. We all agreed that our best player was equal to your best player, you didn't have any one stand out superstar on your team that took out out of the game, and the majority of our team were of very similar skills to yours, in fact our worst players are probably better than your bottom 2 or 3 players. So on paper we should have won. But what we couldn't compete with was the communication between your guys. They just seemed to know where each other were going to be. It was almost telepathiuc. We couldn't work it out. But it was an awesome game."*

What he is was identifying was the result of a unique experiment that we had been trying this season.

Where it began

This is a story about a disparate group of teenagers who, in the space of one soccer season, learnt a lesson that many people never experience or try to understand.

It's the story of the Saints, an Under 15's team, who two seasons prior to this story lost every single game on the entire season. Not most games… every. single. one.

Last season the team managed to finish 5th out of 8 teams. A respectable turnaround from the previous season.

But this year they won every game.

They finished as Premiers with 15 points between them and the 2nd place team. This means that they could have lost 5 games and still been premiers.

They won the Grand Final by 5 goals to 1, and became the champions of their age and division.

Because of their performance throughout the season, they also won a highly coveted trophy from the Football club, and were awarded the highest performing team out of a total of around 800 players and around 50 teams. That's trophy has been a part of the club for nearly 70 years. Their names are now on that shield forever.

Fathers have proudly pointed out their own names on that trophy to their children, and a few players have the great honor of having both their names and their sons name on the trophy, with a gap of 30 years or so. It a big honor. It's a trophy that stands in a prestigious place within the club all year round.

The team won a legion of fans and the crowd they drew for their Grand Final game included onlookers from other teams, coaches from other clubs and fans from the senior teams that had no direct connection with them.

Right now you are rightly beginning to question this radical improvement of this team. They must have been in a different division, one that was beneath their skill level, perhaps they imported a superstar player from another team, or all the opposition players changed substantially. There must be an explanation that makes sense.

But the team remained the same as previous seasons…
The opposition remained the same…
There were not imported players, no future national champions slumming it with the lower ranks.

O.K. There must have been a secret Soccer technique that they learned? One of your players suddenly found his stride and picked up on a technical aspect of his game, which improved everything.

No!

In fact they did not learn, practice or gain a new understanding of their technical game.

No new drills, no guest coach from a professional club, no training camps, nothing was taught to them about their football technique, there was nothing in the traditional sports training that changed which might explain this extraordinary turnaround.

What the hell happened?

Well…. it's confession time.

Playing above the line

This is something even they don't know… until they read it here.

I ran an experiment on them this year. And it was a spectacular success.

Prior to the season the questions in my head went like this….

I could teach them all the game theory, soccer skills and sports psychology that is available and I'm not sure it would help them improve much beyond the normal learning curve.

Could I take the same team as last year and change something which would change the outcome of their season.

Could I give them an experience of what it's like to play in a high performance team?

And is this possible with a raggedy bunch of teenagers?
17 players whose skills levels range dramatically including; 5 players who would have struggled to qualify for a low division school team, 2 players who have previously played at a high level, and a highly creative musician who struggles not say something till until I've finished my sentence, and at least 2 players who have played for less than 18 months.

What is the one thing that could take this sometimes unruly bunch of kids and turn them into a championship team?

Teach them to PLAY ABOVE THE LINE.

I'll tell you what that means soon, but for now, I want to ask you what does it feel like to be a part of a team that is impenetrable?

Have you ever experienced that? At work, home, in sport, at war?

We know it when we see it. But frankly it's a bit difficult to get a grasp on what that hell is happening.

I have read about it in the theatre of war when a group of soldiers came together, never gave up, fought against all odds, and survived.

I've seen it in international sports when an unlikely team pulls together and achieves a result that just didn't seem possible.

I have never orchestrated it in one of my teams before.
I've never done it on purpose, and I've never been in the middle of a championship team until 2014 with that group of teenagers.

It is an experience that will stay with me forever, and has profoundly changed my perspective on teams and the work I do with businesses.

Unfortunately it's a bit like what I imagine a highly addictive drug is like. The experience was so profound that I now judge all other teams by the high that I experienced in this group.

I've taken the red pill, gone down the rabbit hole and there is no going back.

I'm hooked. And I hope to get you hooked too..

Yep, I'm now a pusher for playing above the line. A dealer, an evangelist for this new drug.

When soldiers come back from war they are inextricably connected to each other. Their experience of performing in a unique team holds them together over decades. The same is true of athletes, workers, musicians, even family members who have experienced it too,

It's unbelievably simple and like all things of this nature its deep as well.

How do you know when a team is playing above the line?

Some people describe it as synchronicity.
A fluid interplay between team mates that seems effortless. An intrinsic level of communication that's very, very difficult for opposition to break down and get in the middle of.

This book will tell you exactly how I ran my experiment throughout the season.

It will take you step by step through the laboratory that was the soccer pitch. The failures and the successes. What worked and what didn't.

But this is not just for sports fans.

This is for anyone that works in a team of any type: a family, sports team, work group, band or military unit.

This is for leaders who want more from the people they work with, not just more productivity, but more for the spirit of their charges.

This is for people who want to change the world around them but don't know where to start.

Who this is NOT for....

- If you believe that skills alone will help you win, this is not for you....

- If you think your team won't win without a marquee player, this is not for you.

- If you think that a team of individual champions can take over the world, this is not for you.

Because that is not what my experiment showed.

What my results revealed was that a team, any team, whether highly skilled at their craft or not, can come together to achieve extraordinary results.

The implications of this are quite profound and I'll draw out my learning's throughout each chapter of the book.

My Conclusions;
Take the team you have (no matter what their skills level is) and

teach them Teamwork, not just technical skills and this will create a high performance team where the possibilities are way beyond what you can currently see.
Teach them Teamwork and achieve extraordinary results.

Teach them to play above the line. Teach them to take total personal responsibility for their work and performance and contribution to the team. Show them how to empower every individual in the team, in a culture where they feel included, appreciated and valuable. Teach them to hold each other accountable and eliminate blame, excuses and drama from their vocabulary and thinking.

WHY SHOULD YOU CARE ABOUT THIS?

My day job is running a business coaching practice and I see parallels in businesses all the time.

I see business owners and senior managers struggling to bring their disparate team together and create synergy for their businesses.

I notice how the solution they often go for first is to either work harder themselves to fix the leaks or to bring in an expensive marquee player; a gun sales person, a BDM, or a consultant to fix it for them. They may merge with another business or take on a partnership hoping that this will be the solution to their problems.

The result I see most often is overworked and over stressed people running enterprises that consume their energy and leave them feeling like they don't have any other choice than to do it by themselves.

They struggle to find the right kind of clients and every idea for improvement is met with cynicism and reasons why it won't work. They are constantly disappointed with the people around them and their expectations are rarely met, and never exceeded.

This has a knock-on effect for the lives of your team mates outside of work, with less energy to enjoy the adventures of life and certainly less joy and happiness. They are not resting well and often turn to unhealthy patterns in their diets to keep them going…. so their health suffers.

A feeling of powerlessness creeps in and their thinking often poses the wrong question in search of the right answer. If only this or that changed it would be better… they feel that the power is in someone else's hands to make things better.

This is the total opposite of what it feels like to work in a team with synergy.

If you get it right, what happens is you actually work less. You sleep, rest and recuperate better because you are totally supported by your team mates and you really look forward to working with them each day.

You are tap dancing to work because it gives you energy rather than taking it away from you. New clients seem to appear out of nowhere, and they are dream clients. You hear fantastic feedback from your current clients about your team and everyone is focused on the big goals. The goals that really matter, rather than nit picking over small insignificant things.

People around you will exceed your expectations and over deliver on their promises. They are seeing mistakes as learning experiences and transition into a productive state remarkably quickly after a setback.

Each team member is powerful to create and maintain change, both personal and organisational change.

Because the choice is theirs to make to effect that change.

It's one thing to have book knowledge, as many of us possess, but this soccer team of young people provided life lessons that are now embedded in me at a deeper level than I thought possible.

I hope through their story you'll vicariously get an experience of empowerment and feel the thrill of working in a high performing team, as it turns out, a winning team in every way.

I'm a bit competitive myself, not insanely so, but if there is a challenge I'm keen to dive in and perform my best, and I quite like the challenge of pitting myself against others around me.

But the greatest feeling I've personally ever had in a game is when I've enable one of my team mates to score and have a moment of glory and put the team in front. There is something indefinable about that and it's a feeling that stays with me far longer than the score line at the end of the game.

I've scored a few solo goals myself, outrunning the midfield, getting around the full back and slotting the ball into the corner of the net. But the moments I remember most are when we scored team goals. One of them happened this year when I gathered up a ball that initially looked like it was going out and passed it to one of my good mates who had made a gut busting run. Back and forth the ball went between us as together we outwitted the defenders. Finally, I put the ball past the last guy to put my friend on goal and he nailed it. The back of the net billowed and he punched the air with exhilaration, then came over and high fived me.
He is a defensive back and doesn't get the chance to make a run like that often, so that added to my pleasure even more.

That's synchronicity at work and the reward, for me is much higher than individual glory.

The First Step
The work I do in business has taught me a lot about the science and practice of working in teams and early in pre season I made a decision. I was going to teach them teamwork.

How does it start?
You, the leader just decide to, then get in to action it before you lose your nerve.

I was listening to a friend of mine recently saying the hardest part of any plan is the 30 seconds before you get out of bed. It's easy to just lay there and go about your season the same way you did last year. And you'll likely get the same results.

Playing above the line

So the 30 seconds before you get up you need to play the mental game, because everything starts in the mind. Everything.

Every muscle movement, every thought, every conscious and unconscious action you take in your life starts in the mind. Even before you reach for your tooth brush this morning an electrical impulse would have fired in your brain somewhere allowing your muscle fibers to twitch into action and away you go.

Creating a winning team starts in the mind. It starts with a decision. And someone has to make that decision, so it may as well be you.

Commitment
There is a great poem by William Murray which has gone on to be called The Commitment Poem;

"Until one is committed, there is hesitancy, the chance to draw back, always ineffectiveness. Concerning all acts of initiative and creation, there is one elementary truth the ignorance of which kills countless ideas and splendid plans: that the moment one definitely commits oneself, then providence moves too. All sorts of things occur to help one that would never otherwise have occurred. A whole stream of events issues from the decision, raising in one's favour all manner of unforeseen incidents, meetings and material assistance which no man could have dreamed would have come his way. Whatever you can do or dream you can, begin it. Boldness has genius, power and magic in it. Begin it now."

The very next thing that will happen is that a flood of thoughts will begin to tell you why this will or wont be a success. You'll be flooded with thoughts about making a fool of yourself or the objections that will come up from your team.

My experience is that once I won the battle in my mind about starting, once I conquered the 30 seconds before I get out of bed, the momentum of commitment will keep me going.

So just decide and do whatever you have to do to conquer those 30 seconds every morning.

That's how it was for me. I decided that I'd teach the team to play above the line and that we'd create a code of honour for our team that would keep us playing above that line and we'll see where it takes us.

That's was the first step.

At the next training session I took them aside when we were taking a break, swallowed my fears and started with this explanation.

I said *"I've been thinking about our season and I wanted to introduce you to an idea that lots of the most successful teams on the planet use."* (I know, I'm exaggerating here but I needed their attention)

The most common challenge that arises with teams is unhelpful mind games which have a profound effect on performance and fun.

"Before we start the season this year I wanted to introduce some winning team culture and ideas.

In order to play with the highest level of teamwork, in order to create a championship team rather than just a team of individual champions, there is one important idea that everyone needs to check out, and if you are all open to it, agree to having a go with this."

"Play above the line"

And I drew this out on a big sheet of paper for them so they had a clear idea of what I was talking about.

Responsibility
Laying Blame
Justification & Excuses
Drama

"By playing above the line, we take ownership of what is happening around us and accept the responsibility that goes with it, both in training and during games."

Playing above the line

When something goes wrong, the easiest thing to do is to blame it on somebody else, find an excuse or deny that there is a problem.

This 'playing below the line' is destructive to each player and to the entire Team as it does not resolve anything and problems get worse.

This type of reaction is typical of a fractured and loosing team mentality - failure becomes a self-fulfilling prophecy for people and teams who think like this.

Playing above the line is constructive because taking responsibility for challenges leads to resolution of problems and mastery over the game.

It also ensures that destructive behaviours don't happen over and over again. This pro-active approach is typical of people and teams with a winning mentality.

An essential part of responsibility is taking charge of what you contribute to the environment around you.
Taking ownership of that choice means you accept that your behaviour determines the outcome of any given situation within the team or the game.

This means you have a choice because you own your behaviour and you accept responsibility for your reactions. This is the lesson I learnt in my 20's that has made a huge difference to the rest of my life.

During a game or training you have a choice about how to react, because you alone are responsible for your behaviour. No one else can MAKE you do anything. It is always a choice you make.

For example. You can't stop an opposition player being a jerk. But you can choose how you react to it. You can't choose how a referee will respond in a game but you can choose your reaction to it. Fire up with anger or walk away, it is always, always your choice.

"Would you all be willing to play above the line this season?"

"Yeah!" they all said in unison. I wasn't sure I'd got through to them at all until one of them piped up with a typical, *"Yeah I reckon Josh could do with a bit more of above the line in his game"* – followed closely by - *"Get stuffed! What about you."*

Then about 5 minutes into the next half of our training game I knew I'd got through when one of the team made a typical excuse of why they let the attacker score and someone from the other side of the field shouted, *"that's below the line Josh!"* And everyone laughed, knowing at least they were on a winner to winding Josh up.

Playing above the line

CHAPTER 2.
THE BIG WHY

I think it was somewhere around day 7 of a 10 day training session in Las Vegas that the thought first occurred to me, and it hit with such powerful force it brought tears to my eyes.

What would you do with your days if you were extremely wealthy. If we gave you $500 million dollars right now what would you do with your life? What would you like to be your legacy, the mark you leave behind on the world?

Of course you'd buy some houses, (hell I'd buy an island), boats, planes and some serious toys. I'd have some great fun and I'd look after everyone that was close to me so they could enjoy the fun too.

But after I'd consumed as much as I could, travelled as far as I could and experienced as widely as was possible, met and spent time with some people I found inspiring, and the shine had worn off the toys, my thoughts would turn to *what's next?*

We had been working about 18hrs a day on the training camp and

Playing above the line

I was totally spent. To be honest I was raw emotion. And the thought hit me as clearly as a church bell chime. I want to influence the next generation of young men in Australia to become men of greatness. I want to see provided gender appropriate mentoring for young men and so that they have the opportunity to experience the virtues of being a good man in the new millennium, in the hope that they will contribute something of greatness and lasting meaning to the world around them.

I've seen the education of boys change over the past few decades and I'm quite alarmed by it.

I believe that young men need mentors, and they need them badly. Young women need them too, and I see a lot of work being done for them in schools, communities, in the media and in the public consciousness over the past few decades. This has led to a massive level of empowerment in young women. But I can't help but feel that the boys have been forgotten a little.

We seem to have lost the culture of mentoring amongst men of virtue and noble intentions.

The only mentoring that appears to exist now is of an extreme nature.

Extreme religious ideologies, extreme political positions, health, sport, wealth and lifestyle gurus are only too happy to draw followers to their extreme perspectives. Greater men than me have urged us to avoid extreme ideologies as they very rarely contain the truth or the pathway to a fulfilled life.

The one thing that I believe is true and empowering beyond all other ideologies is the ability to choose for yourself.

I coach young people in sport because it is a microcosm for the life they have in front of them.

The lessons they will learn in a sporting team will potentially help them understand the world that is so rapidly changing around them and provide an education that speaks their language, especially the language of boys.

It is education... but not as we have traditionally known it.

The rights of women have been recognised and have progressed in my lifetime, rightfully taking their place in the commentary and agenda of our world's media and the progress has been stunning. Young women now have the opportunity that is equal to that of their male classmates. There is a great deal of support, education and understanding of how young women learn, mature and view the world and in almost every corner of the academic and business world, those rights have been debated, installed and enacted to give women the equal standing that any modern society, I believe, should afford it's citizens. No matter their gender or race.

This has left the boys a little behind the eight ball in my opinion. I believe that boys learn in a different way to girls, and I believe that the rigid rules and structures of the modern classroom do not suit every boy.
I believe that boys need the influence of strong mentors.
I believe that boys often need to be moving to be learning, or at least engaged in activity.
I believe that boys who find it difficult to fit into academic schooling should have the opportunity to learn in different ways, and I believe that creative thinking and expression are amongst the most valuable assets our children have.
And I believe that traditional schooling and academia does not know how to manage those precious assets.

So I believe that dad's need to be very involved with their children.

It's just not enough to earn a living and provide material comforts for our children, they need leadership, role models and inspiration.

I've seen many of my friends go down this road and I've seen the effects of it on the boys that I've coached over the past 12 years. Absent dads, too busy to be interested seems to make boys who are belligerent, self involved, mean and are contributing nothing to the world around themselves....

In short it's my belief that an absence of strong mentors, and dad's in particular, seems to be contributing to a massive increase in unhappiness and destructiveness in our young men.

Playing above the line

I'm seeing it in the alarming rates of depression and helplessness amongst our teen boys.

I'm seeing it in the senseless violence played out on nearly every news bulletin and the accompanying abuse of drugs and alcohol. The most soul destroying element is the total lack of care or understanding of how their choices and behaviours affect their friends, family, community, themselves and the environment.

What I hear from the young men involved in almost every case is an excuse, an attempt to direct blame at someone else, or complete denial of their responsibility to choose more wisely.

They seem to feel like helpless victims with no idea how to turn the situation around.

Well boys and in particular young teens aren't expected to know how to turn things around. I believe It's our job as men to guide, educate, model, and show the way for our young men to be responsible for their actions, to take ownership of their choices and to be accountable for their behaviours.

And we can't do that if we are always at work, not getting involved with our boys and our community or if we haven't had the chance to understand for ourselves how to play above the line and take control of our lives.

I had the great privilege of encountering a strong mentor in my mid 20's who profoundly changed the course of my life.

He didn't coddle me, or tell me I was right or allow me to get away with blaming others for things I needed to take responsibility for. I was hoping that he'd be a shoulder to lean on and that he'd be an ally to my point of view. I was hoping he'd tell me I was right and the others were wrong.

What I got instead was someone who challenged my thinking without judgment or making me wrong.

I got someone who helped me understand that happiness was never, ever, ever going to come from anywhere or anyone else but from within. That I was capable of being happy no matter what the circumstances surrounding me. And it all came down to one thing.

Choosing my own path and being responsible for that choice. Not allowing others to choose for me. Not allowing what I thought I should do override what was the right thing for me to do. In retrospect I now realise he taught me to stop blaming others for what I didn't have. To stop making excuses for making tough choices and to stop living in denial of what the reality of my choices meant for me.

He taught me to play above the line.

This choice has led to a life more fulfilling than I ever imagined was possible. It has led to resilience in the face of challenge, courage and conviction in my insights, acceptance and a deep happiness for the journey of my life.

It has led to a family of my dreams, A wife who I am more in love with now than ever, and a career that has been a fantastic adventure, taking me all over the world to meet inspiring, famous and amazing people.

I have a balance between my work, my community, my family and my own adventures, and a bit of playtime in there as well.

Every day I wake up saying...I am so grateful.

To give that gift to the next generation of young men I think is what I would do with my life if I was given unlimited money. Because it creates such abundance, generosity, creative energy and happiness.

It gives us power and self determination and can only affect the world around us in a positive way.

Why young men and not young women..... Because there are many others caring for our young women and not as many prepared to care for our young men.

Playing above the line

Because our education systems appear to now be predominantly designed and run by women, great women who I respect more than I can express, but who aren't necessarily appreciative to how boys work. Women educators on the whole appear to like order, calmness, neatness, adherence to the rules and control. In my experience none of those provides an environment where a young man can blossom.

Young men generally like challenge, competition, noise and explosive shows of energy. They like activity and movement and risk taking. They like strong leadership and they like to know their tribe has their back. They like to know they are acceptable as they are…….. smelly, noisy and brave.

Whether that's on a sporting field or in the virtual worlds of games they love challenge, acceptance and to feel valuable.

I've been told by well meaning people my whole life that girls are full of sugar and spice and everything nice.

And that implies that boys are the opposite. This is an attitude that I sometimes see in teachers and school principals.

Boys are something they put up with.

What I believe is that we are all capable of having a profound impact on our world, and that boys, in particular young teenage men, need to experience what it's like to use their natural gifts for good, for leadership and for mentoring the following generations.

I don't yet have that kind of money to have a nationwide impact on the next generation of young men.

But I am determined to give the boys I am in charge of in my soccer team an experience of what it's like to be men of greatness. To give them an experience of what it's like to work in a winning team and to educate them in a way that is meaningful about some of life's lessons that I've been fortunate enough to have passed onto me.

Authors note: You've got to be a champion team, not a bunch of individuals.

This week on a soccer field at a suburban training ground I witnessed the next generation of young men in all their magnificent glory.

I volunteer as the director of coaching at my local club and we have a real focus on encouraging the young men and women of the club to be involved as coaches, referees and in any capacity they want to contribute.

The scene I was watching right now was a young 15 year old coach who was training his under 10's team. He had been in one of the teams I have coached and had experienced the effects of playing above the line, and had heard all the same stories that I'm about to tell you about in this book.

Coaching under 10's is a bit like herding cats, but these young guys really look up to this coach and they are heavily influenced by him. This coach is a great player, highly skilled and wants to give back to his community. He is doing the Duke of Ed program through his school and a part of that is to do some community service, coaching these under 10's was his community service component.... But it can get very draining at times.

He had been teaching them about some of the technical skills of a soccer player, positioning, making space and passing the ball quickly to their team mates. Right now they were playing a game and all that learning had gone out the window as some the players hogged the ball trying to show off their best dodging and weaving skills.

And play broke down. Some kids were getting really frustrated and he could see very quickly this was about to end in pushing and shoving. So he stopped them, called them over and started to give them a chat about creating a champion team. We'll never win as individuals. We need to work together as a team... And then he told the story about the difference between the French team, who were a bunch of individual champions, and the Koreans, who played like a champion team in the 2010 world cup, (you'll come upon that in chapter 6).... And all the 10 year old were captivated.

He finished by asking.. Are you willing to play like a champion team and start setting your teammates up rather than trying to prove how unreal you are? They all responded… Yes coach.

And the next 15 minutes of play were magnificent. He praised the behaviour he wanted to see more of. When someone did a great pass to a team mate they got the full glory of his praise, which clearly meant a lot to them.

These 10 year olds finished the session absolutely electric, high-fiving their coach as they left the field. They had just learned something that very few people get to fully understand.

I was in awe. The next generation wants to make a difference and this young man was doing a brilliant job of it.

And the very best part of it? That young coach was my middle Son.

CHAPTER 3.
DEFINING OUR MISSION

My experience is that teams needed a bigger reason to turn up to training and games each week. So I artificially gave them one.

We created a common goal, our mission, and it was to get to the Grand Final…. Not win it… just to get there. And I saw an immediate increase in energy commitment and fun.

Often, I would be eagerly asked if training was on by my son in the weeks where the weather might mean the grounds were closed.
"The guys at school want to know"
"How come" I enquired.
"Because they're really looking forward to training, they love it and they'll be really disappointed if it's not on." They were pumped.

The first step for our team was to clearly define the result we wanted to see.

It sounds really basic, I know but this was probably one of the most profound things we did as a team.

I started by asking them, *"What do you want out of the season?"*

Playing above the line

Do you just want to win more games than you lose?

Or do you want to have the most fun and not worry about the results?

Is there one team you'd really like to beat?

Would you like to win the Grand Final?

Would you like to just get to the Grand Final?

What the team decided was that we really wanted to get to the Grand Final.

Not win it, just get there.

I think they really wanted a Grand Final experience and the kudos of telling their friends that they made the Grand Final. And in truth I thought even getting there was going to be a long shot based on the past few seasons.

But I figured I could break that down into 2 parts and that football math's would help me from there.

The first mission was to make it to the top 4 semi finals rounds.

In our competition, the top 4 teams essentially start a new competition and play off over 3 rounds for the top 4 positions.

The top 2 play the Grand Final and the winner of the Grand Final is crowned with the title of Champions.

Our initial goal was set. Make it to the Grand Final.

And they put a caveat on it. They wanted to have fun doing it. They didn't want to be hard core and super serious about it. The feeling was that if they were going to be too serious about it then it would certainly take away the fun of playing… There were a few players who felt that winning was more fun than loosing, and there is absolutely no fun at all in being thrashed on the field…so they had to be managed.

In a quiet moment I asked my son, who is a part of the team, what do you really want from the season? His response was that he'd like to win games but in a fun way.

My coaching style has always been positive and I believe what he meant was that they didn't want a coach on the sideline screaming and ranting about what they were doing wrong. I have seen many coaches do this and I have seen the result on the field and after the game and it's not an approach I think works.

So the first goal was to be in the top half of the ladder after the regular season round of 16 games. This meant we needed to finish the regular season in 4th place or better. The previous season we had finished in 6th place and I thought this might not be too much of a challenge.

Then I planned to have them working quite well together and that the momentum would take us to hopefully the 2nd spot where we would have our Grand Final experience. There were a lot of tough teams in the competition from last year and I wasn't under the illusion that we could actually go all the way and win the championship. But getting to the Grand Final was a great goal for the season.

In truth, I wasn't too concerned what their goal was. I just wanted to have them all work towards one thing.
To have a common goal.

I have seen this work time and time again in businesses.
A business that doesn't have a clear common goal will be like a rudderless ship.

People will turn up to work because they have bills to pay and they need some sort of gainful employment, but unless there is a clear common goal for the business, people will not keep turning up forever. Or worse, they will turn up in body but not in spirit.

When that happens, what you'll see is a malaise set in and a gradual slow decline in the business.

It won't happen suddenly, but what you'll notice is things like squabbling over crap that doesn't really matter at the directors meetings, or key staff that you thought would never leave are unexpectedly taking other opportunities and the owners are just letting them go without a fight.

You'll see the owners or directors focusing on profits only, and you'll see them begin to become surely and unsettled, which of course filters right through the organisation.

You'll see customer complaints on the rise and you'll see employees and team members not feel like they have the authority to make important decisions.
These are all symptoms, I believe, of a team without a clear goal or purpose.

I believe that people need a bigger reason to turn up to work or training. We agreed on a common goal to get to the Grand Final…. Not win it… just to get there.
Next the really big questions.
Are you prepared to do what it takes to get there?
Are you prepared for me to coach you and teach you the skills to get there?
Are you willing to be coached in that way and are you really sure you want to commit to that goal?

Yes, yes and yes…. Now can we play some football?

My experience is that management by agreement is a key factor to working with teams.

What that means is ask for their agreement to what you want them to do. If they are in agreement then great.
If they aren't then I'd rather know that up front and deal with it.

I would much rather deal with this right up front. Because if 15 people on your team are in agreement about the goal and 1 is not, then you are in danger of the whole enterprise falling to pieces. They might actively undermine the goal or the leader and they might even sabotage the results.

I've seen a player so caught up in creating attention for himself that he thought nothing of letting the whole team down and allowing a goal through. The rest of the team were so angry at his behaviour that they no longer trusted him in his position. What happens when you don't trust someone.. You attempt to do their work for them and cut them out of the picture, so they won't let you down again.

Then the resentment builds at an alarming speed, the clown will get even more out there in their behaviour, and more team members isolate them, sometimes they even enroll others in a kind of mid-game campaign to take back control, and you very quickly have a situation where you have a number of people actively creating what I call "death the synergy"

This is when a team member or even a few team members are running their own game with it's own rules and it's own scorecard. There is no Synergy in a group like this. No communication, no accountability and you'll see blame and excuses become the primary style of communication. Cliques form, trust erodes and very soon you have a team that is making mistakes that confound even themselves.

I was not prepared to have a team that had even one person not committed, so I asked them as a group and as individuals over the pre season are they happy with the goal we've set ourselves.

A Word About Persuasion

I just want to point out one thing here. I never told them what to do, I asked them what they wanted to do. I didn't tell, I asked.

Why didn't I just tell them what goal I wanted them to have, after all I was the grown up and they are the kids. Isn't that what traditional leaders did? They made up the rules and everyone else followed.

I have found in business that the ultimate sales process is one in which the customer convinces themselves they came up with the idea to purchase the item.

If I encounter a sales person who just hammers me with all the reasons their solution is better and all the reasons I'd be an idiot not to buy, then I just resent them, and the purchase. Why? because they are clearly not interested in whether this solution might be the best fit for me. They are only interested in telling me all their reasons why this is a good purchase.

Let me put it another way.
Lets say you are at an event and you see someone there that you are really interested in, perhaps a really cute guy or girl and you'd love to get to know them a little better, perhaps even go out on a date. So you approach…. then what?

No really what do you do next?
It's not a trick question.
I've asked this question dozens of times and the same answer is always present.

If I was really interested in someone and I thought they were really cute I'd ask questions about them. I'd be interested in them.

If you were on the other end what would turn you off the most. Again the same response. If all they did was talk about themselves I would want to get away from them as fast as I could.

So in a romantic/dating situation you are approaching a reluctant prospect with a sales pitch and you have one of 2 ways you can go.

1. **You can ask all about them and gradually you might both discover that you are a good fit. Result = Next date**

OR

2. **You can sell yourself on all the benefits of you. You can talk endlessly about yourself, your interests, what you like, you can be strongly opinionated on a wide variety of topics and you can share those opinions freely with your prospect. Result = No sale**

Why is it that people believe that persuasion of any description is different?

Amongst many of my close friends who are exceptional coaches, we have a saying; *"the person who asks the questions is the one in charge of the conversation, they are the one who has the real power in the interaction"*

'Ask, don't tell' is the Business Coaches credo. Why? because it is the ultimate sales tool.

Let me show you in an example:
Client: *"Brett one of our guys has said he'd like to move up into a more senior sales position. We really need a new sales guy and we'd like to get your take on whether you think that would be a good idea?"*

Brett: *"Is it o.k. if I asks you a few questions before I answer?"*

Client: *"Sure!"*

Brett: *"What is his DISC profile?"*

Client: *"He is a High S with a leaning toward High C."* (that means he is very methodical and stable and changes very slowly, but when he learns a new skill he will be very good at it)

Brett: *"What profile are your other top sales people?"*

Client: *"They are either high I's to high D's"* (that means they are very outgoing, challenge and people oriented. They act quickly and love to get a yes out of people)

Brett: *"That's interesting. Has he said how quickly he'd like to move into that role?"*

Client: *"Yes, He' like to start working toward it in the next 12 months and be fully moved over in 18 months"*

Brett: *"How quickly do you need someone in that senior sales role?"*

Client: *"Quicker than that!"*

Brett: *"Just based on that do you think he'd be a good prospect for the position?"*

Client: *"No! If he really wanted to move into that senior sales position he'd want it right now, and I'd really like someone who is more eager to get a yes out of people. I'm just not sure his steady nature would work in that situation."*

Brett: *"Sounds like you know the answer to your original question."*

I had a thought that he might not be an ideal salesperson for the role they had in mind. However if I just told them what I think, how persuasive would that have been?

By asking questions that led them down the path to discovery, not only were they totally sold on the idea, but we understood at a deep level what this persons skills were and where they could be best utilised in the team. Just because we needed a senior sales person and he was interested didn't mean it was the right decision for either the bosses or the team member.

Back To The team

If I had told them what I wanted them to achieve would they have bought into it? Probably not, especially since they were teenagers that felt they knew better.

So I asked questions to reveal what they wanted.

What would a great season look like to you guys?

When we are standing here in 12 months time and we look back, what would need to have happened for it to be a very successful season?

What achievement would you really want to hit?
Who would you like to stick it to?
What teams would you like to beat?
Where do you want to finish in the table?
What would you be really proud of?

With each question they argued and discussed amongst themselves the merits of each idea and weighted the pros and cons. I suggested that no idea was off the table, and that we would entertain every option.

After a bit of discussion I attempted to bring the conversation to a conclusion by summing up what they were saying.

It sounds like you are all saying that winning the Grand Final might be a step too far this year, so just getting to the Grand-final would be huge.
Yes!

If we are in agreement then this is the last chance for anyone to speak up if they aren't happy with that.
Are you all totally happy with that goal?

Yes!... *"Now can we play some football"* said our resident smart-arse.

"One last time" I said. *"This means that I'll need to put you in positions to achieve that result that you may or may not like. It means you may not always agree with what I'm telling you, and that if you turn up to a game and you aren't 100 % then I'll give you a rest on the bench. Are you o.k. with that?"*

And with that we had our mission.

What I saw next I have seen time and time again in businesses that I work with where we all agree on a common goal.
A massive lift in energy, focus and determination.

So if you are in charge of a team who are unfocused, low in energy or don't really seem to care about what's happening, I believe the first course of action is to get yourself a challenge... set a goal that everyone agrees on. Then step back and watch what happens.

Ideas start flowing, interactions between team mates increases, synergy starts to appear, sales start to happen effortlessly and opportunities come out of the wood work.

Playing above the line

It seems kind of easy for a soccer team to say we are going to make it to the Grand Final, but what is the equivalent in business, your family or other teams you work with?

CHAPTER 4.
A TALE OF TWO TEAMS

I could feel the frustration and anger rising in me. It started with a slight annoyance, then a grimace at the way the coach I was watching talked to his team but now I was feeling the same as everyone else around me; simmering anger.

We were watching this disgusting display of what was passing as leadership and it was being tolerated by parents, club & officials. This man, who we'll call Mr. X, was pacing up and down the sideline like the wound up angry bear that was about to pounce on his prey. In this case it was any number of unsuspecting 12 year olds on the field in front of us. He barked instructions to his team, unclear, confusing and imbued with a threatening demeanour. It was everything that I find abhorrent in human communications and what was worse, is that my son was out there on the field, potentially subject to his rage.

Every time he yelled at them he took their concentration from what they were doing, they faltered, made mistakes which only increased his anger and frustration and radiated a white heat throughout everyone standing within any distance. I'm fairly sure the opposition parents could feel it too. I have a vision of him on that day hunched over, hands in pocket, foul look on his face and bristling. His mates tried to get through to him to calm him down but with every infraction from his players he drew more and more into himself and the ugly display of emotions and team work got worse and worse.

To balance this, counteract it and probably support the young charges, the parents and supporters on the sideline kept encouraging the players. Occasionally one of the parents would come up to the players on the side line and tell them that they were doing great. But none of that could balance out the leadership style of this particular coach.

The results of this were disastrous. They were down 3:0 and things were going from bad to worse. The typical reaction in any team when this is whats facing you is to avoid being responsible, lest you get singled out for a dressing down. So in Soccer, you just offload the ball quick as you can. And teams tend to pass the ball to the best player on the field hoping they will work their magic and do something to alleviate the pain everyone is going through.

Of course that tactic rarely works. But today a young left back saw an opportunity to do something. He took the ball up the side, played a one two, beating several opposition, rounded another player and hammered home a brilliant goal that he created. The stunned opposition couldn't believe what they'd just seen, and his teams mates erupted with joy and celebration. High fives and congratulations all around. The young player had a smile a mile wide and for a moment there was relief on the sideline. A brief reprieve, or so we thought.

Within minutes the courageous left back was subbed from the field thinking that he was being rewarded with a break for his outstanding effort. The spectators were cheering him as he came off and he was again flashing that beaming smile…. Until he saw his coach. I could see it all happen from 15 yards away. His face just dropped as he caught sight of the white hot rage of his coach, clenched jaw, bloodshot eyes, every muscle repressing a barely disguised explosive anger. And then I saw confusion on the face of this 12 year old player, it was that same thing you see in movies all the time. The moment the victim realises they have walked into a trap.

As he crossed the side line the coach gave it to him with both barrels. *"Why were you out of position? You are a defender. What were you doing up that end of the field? You had no right being there…"* and on and on it went until the cooler head of the manager came over and moved him away. This bewildered young man just didn't know what to make of it and if he had burst into tears no one would have blamed him. But for now his humiliation was just between his coach and himself and a few parents who overheard the whole thing.

Unfortunately after the game during the post game chat, the coach was given another chance to make his point and he was quite merciless in pointing out what each and every player had done wrong and seemed to take some pleasure in letting everyone know that this left back was out of position and he didn't want to see anyone else try that sort of thing.

Rather than celebrate the risk this young guy took and the support and celebration his team mates gave him, or even to acknowledge the lift this courageous action gave the team, he chose to give in to his own demons and dump his crap on anyone that he could. The author Don Miguel Ruiz says that;

'Nothing others do is because of you. What others say and do is a projection of their own reality, their own dream.'

And in this case the coach was allowing whatever frustration existed in his own life to spill out onto these unsuspecting boys. We don't know what he was facing in his own life to lead him to this position, but he clearly did not have the discipline to deal with it himself and he attempted to control every move of the team in from of him. Unsuccessfully.

They were a totally demoralised group of young men and it was on that day my wife and I made a decision to withdraw our son from that team. We didn't want our teenage son to be exposed to such a confidence sucking personality and damaging what little sense of mastery teenagers have. And actually, this was the single identifiable event that motivated me to begin coaching the young team 3 or 4 years ago that is now the amazing bunch of people I am now writing about. So I guess I owe him that.

I never want a young man or woman to be subjected to the sort of treatment I saw that day. In fact, I want them to experience the opposite; the greatness that can come from working in a team. I suspect that everyone can identify with a coach or teacher in their life that has taken this kind of approach. It seems to be about control, ruling with an iron fist and being obeyed.

What I now know through understanding the work of transactional analysis guru, Eric Berne, is that this guy was operating from an ego state of Critical Parent*. This meant that his team were immediately responding to him in child state with either a screw you rebellion or a compliant desperately wanting to please child.

We all operate in different ego states at different times Sometimes rebellious child, sometimes nurturing parent and when we are gathering data and making wise decisions, we are in adult state. I'll go into this in much more detail in the second book of this series.

The Critical Parent is exactly that. Always looking for a reason that you aren't up to scratch, looking to bring you down with "helpful" criticism designed to toughen you up and prepare you for the world. You'll often hear coaches who overuse this style justifying their behaviour as saying it's good for them. Coaches like this will prepare punishments for perceived misdemeanours and tend to put the team into one of 2 ego states themselves, Either compliant child (clearly the most desired state for Mr X) or you'll bring out the rebellious child in your team.

This is after all exactly what you would have done when being scolded by your parents or headmaster when you had broken the rules. The problem with this is that most people aren't aware that they are behaving for this state (or any other) so they don't realise they have a choice. An option to choose another more resourceful style of behaviour for any given situation.

The biggest problem with critical parent is that when it's overused, you find yourself escalating the criticism in order to get the compliance that you want and in the process, creating enormous frustration and anger in yourself and a team member that is either compliant or rebellious. Neither of which will enable them to make good decisions when the heat is on.

The other thing that really upsets me personally is, in the context of competitive sport, it can be quite violent both in language and the actions that follow. I don't think, nor have I seen any evidence, that this contributes to creating a winning team.

Right now I find myself looking across the field at the same coach whose appalling behaviour had led to me being here. He was coaching our opposition team today and his demeanor hadn't changed much since my last encounter with him. The only thing that had changed is that the 12 year olds were now strapping, growing, testosterone fuelled 15 year olds. I wondered if anything had changed, and very soon had my answer.

He was standing on the same side of the field as me and within minutes had become a wound up ball of tension, barking orders at his team and chastising them for not going hard enough. His language became so bad that I chatted to the field marshal, whose job it is to keep cool heads and deal with coach or spectator behaviour when it gets out of order.

The thing that concerned me most was that he was encouraging the players to be very physical and basically hurt my guys to get the ball off them. This led to his team to being highly strung and willing to do pretty much anything to get him off their back. Which they did. Late violent tackles, pushing in the back and verbal barrages at the referee for what they perceived to be infractions against them or unfair calls.

When you are in the middle of this kind of game it gets really spiteful and ugly really quickly. The air of tension that is created by a team who is conducting themselves this way is thick, you can feel it. They commit awful fouls and when you appeal to the referee, or are picking yourself up off the ground slowly after just having the stuffing kicked out of you, they absolutely abuse you; calling you disgusting names and provoking a primitive instinct in you. It's that fight or flight I guess, and in most cases it's fight. It's loud and unjust and it draws you into their universe.

They are often masters at this and the more unjust their barrages, the more the gravity of their attack pulls you into their orbit. It's very, very difficult to resist. And because I am a little protective of my team, and because I find violence so abhorrent, I find myself prone to being pulled in as well. I want to walk over and shake this coach and scream *"do you know what you are doing here? this is ugly and wrong and not in the spirit of the game."* And in my darkest moments I want to scream, *"…and if your team hurts one of my guys on purpose one more time you'll have a volcano on your hands you won't know what to do with."*

I could see my guys getting knocked around. The opposition couldn't keep up with the speed of our passing so they took their frustration out on the players. When that happens, what I see in response is that some of my guys want to take the opponents on in a 1 v 1 battle. I guess they are thinking *'I'll show you'*. My team will hold the ball a little too long and swerve this way and that trying to find space to get some clear air. Occasionally they will get that space and this is where we fall into their trap. Once beaten the opposition will dive at my player, not the ball, and take them out mercilessly. Causing pain to my guys and usually getting issued a yellow card.

All of this just ramps up the ugliness. By 20 minutes into the game the opposition coach was red in the face and nearly apoplectic in his rage. Totally out of control. Screaming *"get them any way you can, hurt them if you have to!"*

Thats the point I made friends with the field marshal. But it wasn't helping.

This style of game was taking it's toll on my guys. We had scored early but their heavily physical game had really made us apprehensive to get the ball, for fear of a giant lumbering opposition player lodging their studs, elbows or whatever other weapons they had into us. We had conceded 2 goals in quick succession. Our tails were down and we were behind going into half time. I could see on the faces of my team that they were battered and bruised and feeling broken as they dragged themselves over to our bench.

They were expecting it by now. The two half time questions;

What are we doing best? *"We are faster than them"*, came the weary reply.

And what do we need to do better? *"We need to pass the ball faster"* Piped up on of the midfielders. And he was right. If we could play one or two touch football they wouldn't have time to get near us, let alone hurt us.

Someone noted that when they are under pressure they turn on each other quite quickly, and when that happens they lose all their shape, everyone starts just chasing the ball and huge gaps open up allowing us to take advantage of the confusion.

Ok, the tactic was to pass the ball really, really fast. To emphasise this, we made a rule. 2 touches of the ball and then offload it. Anymore than that and you'd probably have a huge opposition player all over you.

"What does that mean if you are not the one with the ball" I asked?

"We need to give the player with the ball as many options as we can" came the reply from 3 or 4 players.

"Are you willing to do that even if you are totally knackered?" I said.

"Yes coach."

"What could you do if you can't live up to that promise?"
"we could come off for a rest" they replied.

"Is it o.k. if I remind you?". They agreed amongst the eye rolling.

"You are going to need to really concentrate on being there for each other, giving options, encouraging and communicating. These guys are arseholes and they will only get rougher as we start to come back. Can you handle that?"

"Yes coach"

Mr X was feeling slightly cocky as his team strutted onto the field, they were one goal up and I knew his tactic would be based around shutting us out using their physicality. He would have told them everything they were doing wrong at half time, then urged them to keep up the hard tackles and whatever other nonsense came into his head that he thought sounded tough, relentless, and put his team on notice that he would accept nothing less.

In contrast, I wanted to build belief in my guys and right before they went on, I stopped them. I called them in close and lowered my voice; *"Promise me this guys.. no blame, and no excuses, give everything for your mates and stay above the line…even when you think they are wrong or the ref didn't get it right, be responsible for how you conduct yourselves this half. Play the beautiful game and I am convinced you will outplay them."*

As the whistle blew and the game kicked off I was looking at two completely contrasting teams. Our opposition were tense and their stance aggressive, slightly apprehensive, their sideline was bristling with a combative aggression, the parents were sullen and a little foreboding, as if they knew what would be in store for their boys if they didn't pull this off. On our side the team was determined but lose in their bodies, ready to put their strength and determination to the test. They were alert, their minds were already scanning the opportunities that they could exploit and that seemed to give them more energy. My eyesight isn't good enough to confirm this, but I'll bet there was a cheeky wink amongst them. Our parents and sideline were full of positive encouragement, there was banter amongst the parents and some playful laughter. I was pacing, thinking of strategies and concerned but had been able to resist the pull of their gravitation. We restarted the next half with a restored belief in what we could do and a clear plan about how we would achieve it. What's more, is no one wanted to give up on the goal of going unbeaten for the season, especially not to these turkeys who played ugly football.

Within minutes our hunch had been confirmed. If we just refused to hold the ball for very long and offload it well before they were anywhere near us, we would be safe from their rough play. They couldn't tackle us and, they started to run around like headless chooks chasing the ball all over the park but never quite getting there. Quite suddenly our moment came. The oppositions defence were bunched around the middle of the park trying to shut down a ball that they could never quite reach, leaving our attacking midfielders all on their own down the sideline. The ball was passed very quickly to space picked up by our winger, Percy, and with only two defenders to beat he made a beeline for the goal.

He knew what was coming too, the huge centre backs were going to take him out before he managed to get a shot off, it's all they knew how to do, play rough. But our team saw what was about to happen and moved very quickly to provide support. They did exactly what they promised me they would. They would be there for Percy, they gave him at least three options to pass off to. He crossed the ball low and hard before the centre backs could get him. Their defence just didn't know where to look, they were scrambling back from the centre of the field but not fast enough. In a brilliant display of communication our striker, who would be the obvious target, faked a shot, allowing the ball to roll wide to our right midfielder, who slammed the ball into the net. It was a brilliant team goal and the sideline erupted into spontaneous cheers. The opposition hadn't managed to lay a finger on us and we had evened up the game and the scales of justice. We were winning beautifully.

We managed to put two more goals into the net that half winning the game 4:2. Everyone's tails were up after that comeback goal. It lifted the performance of everyone on that team. The defenders were utterly brilliant, giving everything they had and committing to every play. The ball moved fluidly from backs to forwards and switched from left to right. Not a single excuse was uttered from our side and I heard nothing but encouragement from our team. Praise when someone took a risk and "good effort" when something didn't go quite as planned. They turned small wins into a big win. And they were brilliant.

As expected, the closer we became as a team the more the opposition broke apart. Frustration turned to anger, only this time it was directed at each other, the ref, their coach or anyone they could lay the blame on. Their emotions were high and their intelligence was low. They were being totally controlled by their child ego state and it was running a muck. It is impossible to make a good decision or take responsibility when you are in the highly emotional state of Child, and their game fell to pieces. They started playing as individuals, not as a team, which is exactly what a child does. Take it's bat and ball and stomp around. Only now we had robbed them of the opportunity to hurt us and this just made them more crazy. They did get us once or twice and a few of my guys came off with some nasty stud marks down their legs. But what distinguished us in those moments was a determination to play above the line. learn from our mistakes and make corrections quicker than the other guys.

While the game was a huge victory, the bigger victory was the change in mindset. They chose to play in a way that got them a great result. It all started with a choice, one that was made in a very adult state, considering the facts and assessing what was really going on here. Once they got hold of that idea they were invincible.

It was a victory for me too. Coaching in a positive way and providing a framework of integrity for my players had a far better result than the old school brooding and angry coaching style my opposition was displaying. What meant the most to me was that it made them better men and women that day. They rose up to a big challenge.

After the game, their manager came over to me, who knew me from when my son was playing in their team, and said. *"Wow, we really played your son in the wrong position when he played with us",* (they had played him in the defense and we had him as striker). *"He was sensational today. Your whole team were sensational actually. We thought we had you in the first half but that second half was quite something. A brilliant game."*

Unfortunately, their coach just sulked off, barely uttering a word to his team. I can't imagine what their training was like that week but we would find out how they planned to turn the tables next time, this was in the first half of the season. We would meet them again in the 2nd half, maybe even in the finals.

*A quick and dirty explanation of ego states might help. The human mind is divided into three easily recognised areas, and they are based on the thoughts, behaviours and words we use. Parent state, Adult state and Child state.

In Parent state we make decisions based on thoughts beliefs and behaviours we learned from our parents. What's really contributing to this state is a collection of pre recorded, pre-judged and prejudiced codes for living. And as you'd expect, they are always out of date because you are drawing on information that is about 25 years behind the times. I call these the should's, could's and ought's.

They have a low level of awareness because at this point you are running a program in your head, not actually responding to circumstances around you as they really are. This state is all about control and can be expressed as either a critical parent or a nurturing parent. The child state is the part of us ruled by emotions. When we are making decisions from this state our brain is operating exactly as it did when we were 3 or 5 years old. A child is incapable of either taking responsibility or making a decision. Would you trust your toddler to make a sound decision?

The Adult state is the wise part. It operates like a computer by assessing the data around us, looks for facts and logical explanations and makes decisions based on the information presented. In the Adult state, you have high awareness and you look at the situation in front of you without the limits of prejudice or emotion. It is the state that you can make the best possible decisions and take responsibility for your actions.
Every state has it's purpose. Each one is useful at it's proper time. For example sometimes a parent does need to be forceful to get the attention of children who might be unwittingly wandering into danger. And when we are experiencing great joy and having a lot of fun, we are totally in child state. The trick is to recognise where you are at and employ the right state for the right situation.

Playing above the line

CHAPTER 5.
TOUGHEN UP PRINCESS.
WHEN PUT IN CHARGE, LEAD!

Throughout the season I saw the team achieve extraordinary results. Both as individuals and as a team. I saw the community turn out in droves to watch them play because they knew they were seeing something special. It's something they did, not me. I just gave them the tools to be able to achieve results. They took personal responsibility for what they did with those tools.

I think that many people take on a leadership role because they like having control.

What I experience happens with many who are in charge, is that they either hang onto their control very tightly and do not give their team much say in the job at hand...so they really aren't leading. They are attempting to run a dictatorship or they go through the motions of leadership but never really commit to what it means to lead.

I'm guilty of this myself with the Saints in the previous seasons. I was determined to try something new this season. After all the insanity of doing the same thing over and over again and expecting the outcome to be different is…well…insane.

What I mean by not really committing to lead is that I turn up, set out the tasks and drills to be accomplished, delegate someone to do each task, expect them to do it to the same level of quality that I would myself. I'm often disappointed and then do it myself.

I attempt to keep control by suggesting to the team members that they do it this way or that. When they don't do it just right I am guilty of taking on an "if you'd have done it the way I told you to then you wouldn't be in this mess" attitude.

One of my mentors, Stan Jordan, says to me that the definition of a good leader is that people flourish around them

Let me say that one more time so you really get it...

People flourish around a great leader!

The test, then, of whether you are a good leader is… are people flourishing around you?

In the past few seasons when I was attempting to control through the dictatorship style of leading…No. They didn't flourish.

But when I started to lead in a new way, everyone flourished.

How do I know?…The feedback.

One day I met one of the parents at the local supermarket and they relayed this story to me...

First they identified how energised their son was with the new season upon us. This particular team member was intense, driven, and prone to self promotion and pointing out how much better he was and delighted in telling his team mates what they'd done wrong. But what the parents commented on was about the change in his mindset.

He apparently said. *"Mum, Brett says that rather than just be a team of individual champions we need to become a championship team. That's how we are going to win."*

The fact this guy listened, processed and integrated this idea was a minor miracle in itself. He is, after all an athletic, highly intelligent 15 year old who gives off an air that he knows everything. Of course I had to keep reminding him and his team mates what it means to be a champion team. And what the behaviour of a champion team mate looks like. Especially in the midst of intense pressure. But he was flourishing right in front of me.

I saw the weaker players step up and play amazing games, I saw one of my timid be-speckled players score a critical goal by taking on the responsibility and getting through several layers of defenders, and I saw him grow to a 6 foot giant in that moment. I saw his team mates treat him like the legend he was that day.

I saw the only female team member take on huge opponents and I saw her get the ball away from them time and again. I mean she is about 5 foot nothing (if that) and she took on 6'2" giants.

I've had refs come up to me after the game and say they've never seen a team play with more heart for each other.

I've had opposition coaches tell me that they felt they could match our team for skill, that our best player was no better than their best and in their worst players were much better than our worst players, but they couldn't match our communication and commitment for each other as a team.

I've seen us behind at half time and then come back to devastate the opposition in the 2nd half and the spectators ask, *"What did you say to them at half time"*. Actually, I asked the same 2 questions I always ask;

What are we doing best and what could we be doing better?

After they answered those 2 questions I let them know that they needed to give 100% for each other, if you were walking you weren't giving 100% and you needed to sub yourself off to take a rest, and that I had total belief in them.

I've seen the player who many of the team considered our best have a 5 week absence and we still won and worked brilliantly as a team

I've seen a group of teenagers have the experience of working together in a high performance team. Not just book knowledge but an in-body experience. And I hope that it's an experience they'll take with them into the rest of their lives, perhaps wonder on occasion if they tried some of the things we did in that team with their workmates into the future, would that help them achieve success. Or in their families or in any endeavour they choose to take on with a team.

Most of all, I saw the pure joy of working in a group of people who were in synergy.

And what synergy means is everything seemed a little easier than it should have been because the team were working together seamlessly.

I saw the members of the Saints grow in stature and significance and become more generous and less competitive individually. I saw them absolutely chomping at the bit to get to training or the game. They just couldn't wait to experience this feeling of team work again and again. The fun, the mastery and the competition.

When a team is in synergy either on the sports field, in a family, a band or in business, everything just clicks and together you achieve so much more than you could individually. And you seem to do so with less expenditure of energy.

Many years ago when I was studying science, I learnt a term that is applicable here. Superadditivity.

It's a chemical term and refers to a situation where the result of putting 2 chemicals together creates something that is far greater than the sum of the parts. So in effect 1+1 = 34

That's the best description I have for a team that is in Synergy.

The result of the teams effort is much greater than just the sum of it's parts.

To me, leadership is about putting in place an environment where this type of reaction can happen. When people flourish and the result is greater than the sum of the parts.

But to lead people to this kind of place takes a few things.

Decision + action + resolve = great leadership

Many business owners I've met talk about leadership and the kinds of team they want to create. But to put these into action will often fly in the face of what the spectators and, sometimes, even what your own team mates think. So it takes resolve as well.

Many people want to take the expedient route to success. The most salient option in front a leader is not always the right one for the team.

I can't tell you how many times parents, and team members, even friends have made well meaning suggestions about where I should play certain players to get a better result, or the formation of the team. I'm betting anyone who has coached either professionally or at a local club level often fields these kinds of observations and helpful suggestions.

"You should play this guy up front because he has so much speed, You really need a stronger defensive midfielder…", etc.

What they didn't realise was that I had my own code of honour about how I lead. And that code, I believe, created a team with enormous synergy. I used the materials I had in front of me and I worked to a code that I believe creates not just a better team, but better men and women.

It meant I couldn't just turn up and teach them technical Soccer skills, I needed to teach them how to behave like a team. And to do that I needed to teach them to take personal responsibility for their own production, be accountable to me and their team and eliminate blame and excuses from their game.

Playing above the line

The first step was that I had to make a decision and act on it.

My decision was to teach team, not just technical skills.
And then I had to act on it and put up with all the eye rolling that accompanies teenagers when you are creating change.

I also had to conquer that 30 seconds before I got out of bed, the mind games and all the spectators and doubters that were in my head. And I did this with a philosophy of leadership that was congruent with my beliefs.

What did this style of leadership look like?

Here are a the 21 leadership principals that worked with the team.

1. **Ask don't tell.** Questions are the answers. Dictators tell, leaders ask. My favourite questions to ask the team at half time were these. What are we doing best? and what could we be doing better? I had my opinion, of course but if the team members answered this for themselves and owned what they needed to do in the 2nd half of the game then the results always came. Whenever I've seen a coach just read the team the riot act and tell them everything they should have done, getting all red faced in the process, I've never seen evidence of that method inspiring the team to greater levels of performance. I've only ever seen that lead to frustration, blame and playing dirty.

2. **Manage by agreement.** When I needed someone to do a job I'd ask them if they were willing to do it, and I waited to either get a yes or discuss why they didn't feel they could accomplish the task. There seems to be something different that happens in the brain chemistry when you ask for an agreement than when you just tell an underling to do something. It sounds like this. *'Josh I'd like to play you in a position today that is not your usual position, Are you willing to give that a go?'* Yes coach. *'Are you sure, because I'll need you to hold your position on the right hand side of the pitch and you usually tend to drift all over*

the field, are you sure you are willing to do that?' Yes coach.

When he gets onto the field and he inevitable drifts I don't have to go into long explanations about what he's doing right or wrong and I don't have to get red faced about it either. I just get his attention and remind him of our agreement. And in most cases, just getting his attention reminds him of what he's agreed to do and he's back on course. I use the same methodology when I'm asking my children to clean up the kitchen after dinner. Of course they don't want to do it but I ask if they are willing to do it, get a yes or a genuine reason why not, then double check... are you sure? Then if it doesn't get done I just ask why they haven't done what they agreed to do? I don't seem to get excuses and it's not inflammatory in any way. It's just an open and upfront agreement about what they are willing to agree to and they are clear on what the expectations are.

3. **Praise the behaviours you want to see more of.** I learnt this when I was coaching under 6's. Heap praise on them when they exhibit the behaviours you want to see. For example; I will praise the crap out of the player who assists a goal more than I'll praise the goal scorer. I figure they have the pleasure of finishing off the goal anyway, but without the work of the players that assisted the goal, that glory would not have happened. I do this in businesses as well. The sales guys so often get the praise, but without the admin and support team that sale would never have happened. Make sure everyone who contributed to the goal get a share of the glory. That way you'll see it again. There is nothing more frustrating in a soccer team than the guy who won't pass off the ball but must go for glory, and miss, when his team mates are standing there with an open goal. Just pass off the bloody ball and share the glory. To lead your team to this you must, must, must praise the assists.

4. **Do not give positive attention to the behaviours you want to see less of.** Use time outs to maintain this discipline. There are always those in your team who absolutely must have the attention on them. I've been coaching boys like this for more than 10 years and it can

be enormously frustrating when they redirect the attention from the task to them. If you react to this you are giving them what they want… Attention. So exclude them until they are prepared to play by the rules… then praise the crap out of them for playing by the team rules.

5. **Be absolutely clear about what behaviours you expect to see and do this by asking them questions.** E.g. Is that how a team member of a champion team would talk to his team mates? Unless you give clear direction about what a great performance looks like then how will they know? Does my team know what a great performance looks like? Do they know what the definition of "great" is? If not, let them know.

6. **Create a common goal that everyone is committed to and gets excited about.** This is a foundation of all great teams I believe, and I'll go into it in far more detail shortly, but without it I don't believe you have a reason to improve, change and come together as a team. Its the glue that holds the whole enterprise together.

7. **When put in charge….. Lead.** Decide and act as quickly as is practical. Don't hold back, because this is one of the critical points. If you aren't sure how to lead effectively then learn, quick. And learn from anyone you can, mentors, other club officials, books, films, anywhere that inspired you to take action and help those around you flourish.

8. **Design a set of 'Rules of the Game'** that governs the internal behaviours of the team and create a code of Honour that's right for your team. This must start with the leader, because mostly the team have no idea why this is important or how it will benefit them. But once you have created the rules it's vital that everyone on the team buy into them, so tweak them if necessary, but everyone must agree to play by these rules or you are going to have trouble.

9. **Make work fun.** Make learning fun. Your team will keep up

the discipline of the weekly grind if it's wrapped up in some fun activities. I never ever did drills. Instead, I got straight into a game and got them doing the drills within the game. I manipulated the teams so that different players got to work with complimentary players that would help on game day, rather than just playing with their mates. As you'll see next, I always rewarded them at the end of the training session by allowing them to play with their mates... the swallow the frog principal.

10. **Swallow the frog first.** If you have a task that you need your team to do and it's not as pleasant, do it first. Save the fun stuff as a reward for the team after you've done the hard stuff. For example, I would make the team play limited touch football, where they are limited to 2 or 3 touches before they must pass off the ball, before I would allow them to play unlimited touch where they could show off and do the glamorous stuff.

11. **Make it competitive.** If there is nothing to win and play for then the intensity is not as great. Several times I would finish the training sessions with a world cup between 3 teams. So right off the bat the intensity of the games increased. Then I put a time pressure on each of the rounds. Maximum of 6 mins and I reminded them of the score and the remaining time as we counted down. The effort, commitment and work rate increased massively as the pressure to get to the next round increased.

12. **No team comes together unless they are under some sort of pressure.** This is the principal of perturbation*. In a sports team each game day is it's own form of pressure. So too is the pressure of achieving a goal that seems unattainable. If you don't have an outside force providing pressure it's important as a leader that you get some if you want your organisation to reorder into a stronger state and become more adaptable to ever-changing environments. This is why coaching is so effective as a model for change. It is an outside force providing pressure for change and improvement.

13. **Play the game with honour**, respect your opponents (no matter what), never, ever, ever question the ref or officials. Play in a way that you, your supporters, family and coach are proud of.

14. **Mistakes are a learning experience**, fix them quick, move on and accept the lesson. I was once trained by a former Brazilian National professional player. He said to me in a candid moment that he couldn't understand why us Aussies beat ourselves up for making a mistake. Just fix it as fast as you can and move on. What this means in the middle of the game is, no tantrums or throwing your hands up in the air in frustration, or mouthing off at the ref for a perceived infringement. Just get up, chase down that ball and get back in the game. Every second you spend beating yourself up is a second you are not contributing to your teams game. You may as well be sitting on the sideline at this point.

15. **Give 100% or get off the field.** If you tell me you are ok to play then I expect you to give 100%. If you can't, then tell me. It's O.k, but I need to know. There is nothing so frustrating as unmet expectations of your team mates. As a leader that means you need to commit 100% to where you are leading your team, stand up against the uninformed opinions of others who think they know better, stick to the course your team have agreed on and give it everything you've got. Or let them know you are not up to it and go to the bench to recuperate.

16. **Reward and support risk taking.** Without someone willing to take a risk we don't move forward. In the Australian culture we like to take the piss out of people who take risks, and remind them of how they did it wrong and how they could do it better. I feel that's just blame wrapped up in a cultural norm and it's destructive. So I like to install a culture of support for risk taking, and if it doesn't work out so well, then we still support the attempt. This happens in a game when a midfielder decides to take on the defence and go for goal, but misses and bases the ball over the post. Rather than berate them with supposedly well meaning jibes, I want to see recognition for having a go.

This fosters a culture of support and allows team members to give more when it matters

17. **Take the team you've got and teach them to play above the line**** Teach them to take responsibility and ownership for their contribution and eliminate blame and excuses from their vocabulary and thinking.

18. **No team member will ever feel unsupported, ever.** They will know that I have their back no matter what and that my greatest desire is that they grow as a human, not just win a game. Create an environment that every team member know that they are supported. We win as a team and we lose as a team. This is vital and contributes more to a team breaking down than most other elements. If you feel like you have been hung out to dry by either your leader or a team mate then that trust will be very difficult to repair. Some personality types (I'll introduce you to those in a following chapter) will require you to maintain that trust, otherwise you'll never get the performance. One breach of trust and it's over.

19. **True communication is the response you get from your team.** If your team are communicating with you in a way you don't like then first have a look at the way you communicate with them, it's probably a reflection of how you communicate with them. The same principle is applied to the team mates. If they are putting down others then the communication that will reflect back to them will be likewise destructive. You are ultimately in control of the communication you receive from others by initiating it in a way that you would like to have it reflected back to you.

20. **Transition from one state to another as quick as possible.** In Soccer, the concept of transition relates to moving from a defensive phase of play to an attacking phase, or vice versa. That is where a counter attack comes from, but it takes preparation. If you are not ready to transition quickly the advantage will be quickly lost. Likewise if you are attacking, and play breaks down, you

are not ready to transition to a defensive mode quickly then you will quickly concede. But I like to extend the concept of transition to every part of the game; mindset, physical rejuvenation, injuries, the officiating of the game, preparation - everything! The faster we can move from an unproductive state to a productive framework then the faster we can adapt to the ever changing environment. The exact same principle is evident in business. Things won't always go your way, but the faster you transition from a defeat to a more resourceful approach the more quickly you will grow. Likewise when you get a big win, the faster you can transition to a mode of protecting that win and satisfying customers expectations then the more wins you'll have.

21. Never, ever, ever give up!

Perturbation: definition: The deviation of a system, organisation or living structure from its regular or normal state or path, caused by an outside influence. E.g. These shifts and swings in wildlife populations are possibly related to climatic perturbations.

The effect of perturbation on an organisational structure (a team for example) is a disordering process. Once the organization begins to disorder it will likely reorder into a stronger state, better able to withstand greater pressure. The team, or organisation become s stronger, more resilient and can take on greater and greater challenges. This happens in nature all the time and is the process by which we say that a living organism is either living or dying. It is constantly undergoing pressure to grow or disorder and die. There is no status quo in nature and increasingly we see in teams, businesses and organisations that this natural law is at work too. A team is either growing, changing, adapting or it is in the process of disordering, disintegrating and decaying. So I believe that the only choice for a team that wants to at least maintain their performance is to decide to improve. Innovation, change and improvement is the fuel that keeps a team at status quo. Increased pressure and lofty goals will keep a team motivated to greater levels of performance. A lack of any of the above perturbation will see either a rapid disordering of the team or worse a slow painful dismantling of a once great team, business or organisation. Lifetime learning is what I believe you must commit to if you want to maintain the perturbation process for your leadership and your team. It never stops. Just go to bed a little wiser than you woke up, and day by day you will achieve unimaginable success, according to Charlie Munger.

** A lot has been said by highly successful managers about having the right people on the bus. There is a belief that having highly talented players would make your job as a coach so much easier. I must admit that in the past I've said to myself "if only I had a player who could….. "

Jack Welch in his book "Winning" suggests that even a good enough player isn't good enough for a high performance team. You need top performers on your team. But I didn't have that luxury. I had a team that had players of various levels of skill. I had a few players that were division 1 level, most who were about division 4 or 5 and some who might have struggled in division 7. My role as a leader was to highlight the strengths of each player and utilise it to our best advantage, but more than that I needed to educate the other team members on that skill and provide an environment where they could be praised for that contribution by the rest of the team. What I found was that the lower skilled players contributed far more than I expected, and their performance far exceeded expectations. For example; we had one player who is a little bigger than the others, and a little slower too, not always as naturally coordinated as the others, but he was strong and keen. So we encouraged him to use his strength and he threw himself into it, putting his body on the line and getting up smiling each time with his team mates helping him up and congratulating him for his effort. The most athletic players regularly praised him at half and full time and the more they did the more he gave. I believe that it took a willingness to do that by him but the evidence is that as a leader, finding the uniqueness in your team and working out how to use that to contribute to the team is a highly rewarding process for everyone involved.

Playing above the line

Readers Report: Creating a winning mindset

A report from a regional sales manager at a multinational electronics business

The idea of coaching our team rather than just managing them really took hold in our organisation. It was such a new perspective. And the effect was quite significant.

We have team members right across the Asia-Pacific region and it was quite difficult to keep everyone motivated, and connected. Especially in the isolated areas.

One of the most influential things we did was to ask our team to identify and report on 3 Wins each week.

A win is something that you feel good about achieving. It can be a small personal thing, such as sticking to a diet or loosing some weight, or large and business focused like a progress on a huge business deal, or reactivating an old client.

What that did to our team was to get them focused on what was going right in their lives and their work, rather than focus on all the hurdles and difficulties.

Week after week we asked them to write and report on their wins to their team mates. Sometimes it was just by email, other times we did conference calls. But either way when we had meetings the first thing out of their mouth was a win for the week. It totally changed the culture of our organisation. They weren't complaining to me anymore about all the things that were wrong, or difficult, or resources they didn't have. Instead they usually wanted to tell me and their teammates about their wins. The whole mood of the organisation changed. It became very positive, and the business results improved as well.

Authors note:
Using the 3 wins is a regular part of dealing with your team, and it's such a simple idea. It almost seems too simple.

But the impact is profound.

When I'm working with a team who want to move from problems focused to solutions focused, one of the first things that I do is to get them oriented to a winning mindset.

The effect of a winning mindset is profound. In sport we see it's effect all the time. After our team scores a goal we feel invincible for the next few minutes. We suddenly believe that we can score another goal. And often do white quickly. Many games have gone for 60-70 minutes without eater side scoring a goal and once that first goal is done 3 or 4 often follow in quick succession. A winning mindset is what makes the difference. The same players are still on the field but I am often looking at a different level of play.

In organisations and in regular team meetings what gets attention is often the things that aren't going right.
And what Psychologists tell us is that behaviour that gets attention gets repeated. What ever we give most attention to will be repeated.

They call a unit of attention a "stroke". And whatever you stroke (give attention to) you will see more of. When we start our meeting off with a focus on wins then this kind of focus is what gets repeated. Winning behaviours and winning mindset is created and enforced week after week. Pretty soon your whole organisation has a winning mindset and are leaping over hurdles that once stopped your team in its tracks.

One of the unintended consequences of doing the 3 wins exercise is that team members start to deal with their own problems rather than bring them to a manager for endless un-resourceful chat. It is an important building block in creating a winning culture and a far more independent workforce.

Playing above the line

CHAPTER 6.
PLAYING ABOVE THE LINE

"I don't know what you said to those kids at half time, but the comeback in the second half was…I don't know…I'm lost for words… Legendary. We thought we had you on the ropes at the break but clearly I was wrong." Is exactly what the opposition manager said to me at the end of one of the most memorable games I ever saw our guys play.

We knew these guys would be tough, they were 3rd on the ladder but were really scrappy, tough fighters. We had only beaten them by 1 goal in the previous encounter, and that was a late header. They defended well and were quite physical, which tends to put many players off. We went down a goal early. Which gave us a shock, but we've come back from there often, it's not that far back. But in quick succession we went down another goal, which knocked the team off their perch, and then shortly after that a mistake in defence meant we were down 3 nil at half time.

This was the situation I'd been waiting for in our season to see what we'd really learnt. Would we descend into chaos and lose the discipline of playing above the line or could we keep it together. We had a very solid agreement in place for our team about how we would behave in just this kind of situation. High emotion low intelligence, I'll tell you more about it in an upcoming chapter called creating a "Code of Honour". What it meant was we weren't going to play dirty and be overly physical in response, no revenge tackles. We weren't going to start arguing with the referee and we were not going to start yelling and swearing at our team.

On the other hand, the opposition coach was loud, angry and aggressive. Yelling, "Take them out if you can't get around them", and screaming at his team with biting instructions of what they were doing wrong. I thought this was fairly offensive and asked a club official to go over and calm him down a bit. But at the half time break his hyper aggressive approach seemed to be working, my team came off the field with their heads down and looking beaten. 3:0, we'd not found ourselves in this position all season. Behind by an almost insurmountable lead.

Half time is a high pressure time for a coach and a team. We've got about 6 minutes to get the players hydrated, rested and reorganised. The approach I use is the same as they use in one of the great clubs of the world, Barcelona FC. When they are down, take care of their emotional wellbeing. Learn from the mistakes and move on quickly. No recriminations, no justifications. Just corrections and action.

First just the facts.

What are we doing best?

What could we be doing better? A few people begin to offer answers but, unusually I do a bit more talking at half time on this occasion.

"The thing you could be doing better is committing 100%. Not just to the game but to your team. Some of you are walking, some out of position, others are not backing up to support your team mates.

What could we do to make certain that everyone in this half commits everything to the team?" They started speaking up now.

"We could talk to each other more." Andy you are in charge of the mid's and forwards, Eddiey are you willing to take on the team talks amongst the defence? Is everyone willing to start talking more positively and often? *"Yes coach."*

"We could move quicker into space, us midfielders could organise our defence and attack better." Chimed in another

"We need to rest more often," said someone else

"We need to stay above the line."

"And we need to move the ball faster so they can't hit us with those heavy tackles." Said one of our attackers.

"Midfielders that means you can only take 1 or 2 touches maximum, Are you willing to do that?" I said.

"Yes coach."

"Are you willing to give 100% for your mates, stay above the line and make sure no one is left unsupported?"

I sent them on with a little speech that was 50% about firm discipline and what performance I expected to see and 50% about belief. The discipline…*"Don't just say you are going to do it, either really commit to it or get off the field so someone else can."* Then the belief… *"I believe you can win this, your passing and teamwork is the best in the division. You can only win this as a team, not as a bunch of individual players and when you do it will be the sweetest victory you have experienced."*

After a few minutes I knew we were looking at a different team. About 4 minutes into the game one of our midfielders scored an amazing goal putting himself totally on the line to finish a brilliant team goal. He finished on the ground in a heap of bodies and dust and I saw 4 of our players run over and haul him off the ground, nearly into the air with the sense of excitement and joy, and then high fives and hugs all around. This was a different team and I had a sense something really special was about to happen.

Buoyed by the superhuman effort of that first goal they scored another brilliant goal from a gut busting run from our winger finishing with a huge cross which was met at the back post by the head of our striker. Fast movement and an almost telepathic communication get us that goal. The equalizing goal looked almost identical but from the left this time.

By now the opposition coach was not so noisy, in fact he was rather silent. He'd just seen a 3 goal lead reduced to nothing. His team were starting to bicker and argue, yelling at each other and blaming this person or that. They were becoming more fractured and separate, fast becoming a bunch of individuals and no longer a team. They were quickly loosing the quality that helped them get 3 goals against us in the first half. They knew it and my team certainly knew what was happening. We were coming together as a winning team whilst the opposition was breaking apart.

The final goal came from the entire team. Our right back, who is a slight, thin boy, is also one of the most determined players I've met. He put himself on the line to stop a big attack, never letting up on his opposite number who was 15cm taller than him and using his extra weight to "take out" our defender. But he never gave up and managed to hustle the ball away.

What happened next was so fast that it left everyone speechless. The ball moved swiftly in a series of one touch passes though most of our team. The opposition couldn't keep up, they were chasing the ball, but as they thought they had closed it down, we moved it onto the next player. Each player readying himself for the next pass as their team mate received the last one. The final movement set up our smallest player, Hayden for a magnificent opportunity. He still had to beat 2 defenders and a goalie all of whom were taller, rougher and much angrier than he was. Surrounded by the other forwards who were on hand to support and collect any rebounds Hayden calmly rounded the defenders and put the ball into the top left hand corner of the net.

It felt a little bit like a movie.. First stunned silence for a few seconds…. and then in unison everyone on our sideline, every parent, brother, sister, grandparent and spectator roared into life. Hugging each other, cheering and screaming from the top of their lungs. It was pure delight, pure joy.

We finished up wining by 1 goal.

I was privileged to be watching a legendary performance from a legendary team. I might have given them the tools to work together as a team but their commitment to each other, their willingness to stay above the line and never dip below it is what created the legendary win that day.

I thought I wouldn't see another game like this during the season, but I was wrong. We would go on to greater and greater things this season, and it all started with the simple idea of playing above the line.

Here is Johnno's Match report from that game.
Saints 4-3 Easts

A great game of football.

In the early stages of the match, The giants were looking strong. We knew that this was likely to be the case. Our defence stayed solid for the most part, however there were some shots on goal but Jack made light work of them and kept them from entering the dark depths of our net. It was not all Easts in the first minutes though, with Andy, Diago and William all looking like putting the ball into the back of the net. Our defence was pressured heavily but stood strong, but not quite strong enough with Easts getting through on goal a few times and slotting a couple past Jack. A couple of goals down, a situation rarely encountered by the "Legendary" team (quote Brett Odgers). It went from a rare *experience to a completely new experience in a matter of minutes. Easts broke through again. Goal to Easts. It was the time to welcome the sick *lazy* Hayden to the field. Anyway, moving on. The rest of the half was tight and was nip and tuck all the way to the whistle.*

(For this game we only had 12 players, and 2 of them were quite sick from a bad virus that had swept through he school that week, one of our players had a birthday party the night before not getting to bed before 3am so
 his lethargy was self inflicted)

Second Half

I don't know if it was the way I cut the oranges or if there was something in them but we seemed to come out screaming in the second half. The first of our goals came from a wonderfully worked piece as William crossed the ball in to Andy who tucked it away in an honorable fashion. The second goal from the lazy… I mean sick Hayden was about the worst kind of goal you can score, however, he was feeling lazy, or sick, so it was a big achievement for him. It was time for William to get in on the action in this crazy goal frenzy. A great ball from Diago set William up for a strike of which Heskey would have been proud. Then we followed with another goal that started with our back and very quickly worked it's way through nearly the entire team before being slotted home. Again, there was a period were it was neck and neck, both team fighting for possession. It looked to be a fantastic comeback from the Saints. And it was a spectacular goal that put us in front in the dying minutes of the game.

A thrilling match it was.

MOTM - Andy, again…because pace (The coach would have chosen Hayden for playing while half dead from a virus and still managing to score)

Special mentions - Thomas for always covering me when I went up and Diago for never letting his annoying team mates get on his nerves.

Playing Above The Line: a brief explanation.

Being the title of the book I wanted to show you in a bit more detail what this meant to us in our team and how we used this philosophy to change the course of our season. I make use of this idea in my own life and in the work I do, and I'll go into it in much more detail in my next book, but for now this is how we understood playing above the line.

When you play above the line, you take responsibility for the issues you typically agree to be accountable for to your team for what you contribute. You are also taking responsibility for your attitude and your contribution. You are choosing to have the power for change and choosing how you behave within the team.

When you play below the line, you lay blame on others for the result, you justify why things happened the way they did and that leaves you in an unrealistic situation as to the true cause of any given situation and the potential remedies.

Simply put, this is what it looks like…

RESPONSIBILITY

_____ (the line)

LAYING BLAME

JUSTIFICATION

When you choose to approach life, it's hurdles and issues from the perspective of playing above the line, this contributes to personal power. No matter what the issue facing you is, you can take ownership of it, make corrections and change the course of the future.

In a team environment this requires every member of the team to commit to this idea. If even one person holds out, starts playing below the line and is unwilling to move, then you have a victim mentality.

Why a victim mentality? Because when you blame others or circumstances for the result you got, do you have any power to change that?

I hear it all the time in businesses. The economy is bad this year. Customers just aren't putting their hands in their pockets. I can't just make people buy what we've got. I can't afford the solution I really need. I'd like to but...(insert excuse here). My staff just aren't up to it.

Playing below the line means you look to place the blame for your results with someone or something else, you often end up making excuses and justifications for what things haven't gone the way you hoped and that often leaves you in denial as to the real causes of the failure. All of it adds up to a total lack of power. Lack of any ability to effect change for the better because you have handed over that power to another force that's outside your control.

One of the things I hear within organisations all the time is that people feel they don't get paid enough and they feel powerless to earn more money in their current job. Another one is that people don't feel they have enough time to get everything done. If only I had more time or more money or better staff or less demanding clients or a better quality clients or……….. you get the idea.

The second you put the words "if only" or you preface what you are about to say with the word "but" you are playing below the line.

If you want to be paid more money it's quite simple. Be worth more money. This was the wisdom of Jim Rohn. Be worth more money and sell the kind of stuff that people really want and sell it to them in a way they really want to receive it.

Charlie Munger of Berkshire Hathaway said it quite clearly.

"The safest way to get what you want is to deserve what you want. Deliver to the world what you would buy if you were on the other end."

I highly recommend you memorise this and make it your life's motto. It is the ultimate form of playing above the line.

If you want to be captain of the sports team then deserve it. Lead in a way that other people would follow. Become the person that you would like to follow yourself.

During our pre season I was taking our guys through some sessions and I gave them a task to complete. It was a world cup task. They had 5 minutes to score more goals than the others. I asked them to appoint a captain of the team and immediately one of the ultra confident members in the team piped up and said the search was over, he'd be the captain. Reading between the lines I could see that this boy felt he would be able to boss everyone around and put his favorite friends into the positions he felt they should be playing in (because no one else knew as well as he did, especially not his coach or team mates).

So I asked the remainder of the team. Would you be happy with this guy as your leader? Would you follow him? Silence, shuffling feet. That's teenager speak for no way, not on your life.

Who would you follow then? They all pointed to Andy. A quiet, but confident young man. You'd all be happy to follow his lead? Yes coach. O.k. I'll leave you to sort out a strategy, You've got 2 minutes till kick off.

As I walked away I saw everyone listening to Andy, lots of nod's. I saw our pretender leader sulk a little, arms folded shuffling his feet, but he gave in quite quickly and decided to let his athleticism do the talking in the game.

Andy deserved to be the leader and everyone could sense it.

Playing above the line

When I look at him I often wonder what it is about people like Andy that makes them natural leaders. I can only go back to what Charlie Munger said. Andy was always the kind of team mate that was a joy to coach. He was open to new ideas, he was insightful and took responsibility immediately. He was justifiably proud of his own efforts but he wasn't rubbing it in anyone's face. On the field he was always one of the first to go over and congratulate the goal scorer with a hi five and he often acknowledged the assist as well. If he scored off a brilliant assist, which happened often, he immediately went over to thank his team mate that provided the assist.

He calmed down the tempers on the field and he took responsibility for chasing down the difficult ball and making the gut busting run.

I noticed that he was a learning machine. He had ideas and strategies he wanted to talk about but didn't assume he was always right.

When we played a three way world cup I often coached the team on the sideline with me to become coaches. To look at the game and asked them what would they change to get a better result. Andy was attentive and made thoughtful suggestions.

Andy went on to do his referee's certificate and spent much of his season working a ref. Which gave him a very deep understanding of not only the rules of the game but the psychology of the referee adjudicating our games.

Rather than just watch premier league football on TV, Andy took on the responsibility of learning as much as he could about the game from any source he could.

He deserved leadership, and everyone around him knew it without him needing to explain why.
He played above the line with leadership and we made him our captain for the season.

There is huge pleasure in life to be obtained from getting deserved trust. And the way to get it is to deliver what you would want if the circumstances were reversed.

What does it look like when you play below the line on a football team?

Two words: Blame & Justification

These elements in any team means death to synergy.

Justification & Excuses

What did it sound like in this team?.

"Coach I was too tired to get back and help"

"It's not my job to do that, I'm a forward I'm not supposed to go back there."

"I had just done a run up and couldn't get back in time."

"Why was I out of position? I wanted to chase the ball down."

Laying Blame & Justification

This is where most teenagers seem to live. In fact, I hear many, many people I've met, in all areas of business and life, blaming and justifying why stuff hasn't been done.

My unsuccessful friends come up with justifications all the time. The economy has gone off, the market has changed, my team aren't performing, clients are so price sensitive they won't pay what I need.

I almost never hear it from very, very successful people.

In businesses that are struggling I hear all elements of not taking responsibility; the brief wasn't clear, I don't now what they want me to do about it, they aren't telling me the truth, now they are angry and they won't talk to me, my team aren't delivering what I need...

Justification. Its the opposite to empowerment of the problem.

Playing above the line

How do you get out of Justification? Just say this sentence;
"if it's going to change, it's going to be up to me to make that happen"

You know you are about to descend below the line when you hear the word BUT…... or the phrase IF ONLY.

Any sentence that starts with the word 'but' means you are highly likely to hear some blame or an excuse.

Below The Line At The World Cup

I wanted my team to have a clear example of what happens when this works well. Being enthusiastic young players they followed the big teams and the big names and I knew a story from a World Cup that I thought might help clarify the concept for them a little more. So one night at the drinks break of training I told this story.

In the 2010 world cup of Soccer/Football the French team were amongst the highest paid team in the history of the sport.

The combined salary of the team was unbelievable. They had the best of the best. Their team had so many champions that they felt they were a certainty for world cup glory.

The team recruiters must have been patting themselves on the back for putting these guys together.

Individually, the players were jaw dropping. Big, big names who were paid 100's of millions of dollars to play the beautiful game. They played for the top clubs in the world and for the top coaches. The expectation of the spectacle was immense.

Do you know what happened to them that year?

For the first time in their history they were bundled out of the competition in the first round. They left the tournament in disgrace with the arguments, blame and recriminations making headlines around the world. The coach was fired and I don't think they ever played together again.

The players were blaming the management, the pitch the draw, the weather. The management were blaming the players claiming they were playing power games. There was a total disconnect between both groups and it was evident not only at the game, but at trainings, press conference's, everywhere.

They left the country as soon as their final defeat was done, with some players even leaving that night.

When they arrived home they were under a barrage of media scrutiny, recriminations and an outpouring of frustration and anger from the French public who they were representing, and I can't image how long it must have taken for some of those players to recover.

I would have expected that their performance at club level would have suffered for a while after such a toxic exposure.

What the hell happened?
So much promise, so much talent and it led to nothing.

The media reported nothing but excuses, players blaming the management and the coach reciprocating. Heated arguments ensued and it spilled over onto the field.

It certainly looked like a team playing below the line and taking no responsibility for turning it around.

There was another story that year. The Koreans.
They were not favoured at all. They were ranked very low as a nation, yet they had a phenomenal year and finished 3rd in the competition.

No super stars, no tantrums, just a clear code of honour that bound them together to achieve something amazing.

The French..... a team of individual champions.
The Koreans... a championship team.

Playing above the line

No Blame, No Excuses, No Justification.

This is how I wanted to embed the above the line ethos into our team. It was simple and they understood it.

If you are too tired to run down the ball, get off the field and have a rest. We have unlimited interchanges in our competition and 5-10 minutes on the sideline to regain some hydration and take a break will do wonders for your performance.

If you are on the field and not doing your job then I believe you are letting your team down. If you can't run, get off the playing field and rejuvenate.

Nothing drives me more crazy than having a player beg me to get on the field and then play wherever they want, out of position, not making an effort, not backing up their team mates and unwilling to get off the field. It is the ultimate below the line behaviour. You are in denial of what it takes to be a productive member of the team and when I ask people like this, "what's going on" guess what I get in return... Blame and excuses.

If you are walking, out of position or not backing up your team mates then you are a spectator, but you are taking up the position of an effective member of the team.

I would much rather have a player say to me I'm not 100% today coach because then I can put a strategy in place to account for that. If they are tired, then encourage them to contribute in short bursts of effective activity and then rest.

If you turn up late or you couldn't find the ground or any number of other reasons why you are not where you should have been, I just don't want to hear it. I'll expect you to go through a full warm up and if that means you are not available to play until the second half then that's what it means.

I know things happen that people feel are out of their control, but are they really? If I've asked you to be at the ground 45 minutes prior to kickoff and you have never been to that ground before, do you think perhaps you should leave a little extra time to find it? Just in case.

If one of the boys had stayed up until 2am playing computer games and they were not fully awake at the field that morning, who is really responsible for that?

If you are out of position and I ask you why and you start telling me it's because of this and that and start pointing to other players you are below the line and I don't want to hear it.

If you are tired. **Rest!**

If you are uncertain. **Ask for help!**

If you don't think you can deliver. **Tell me up front!**

If you disagree with the referee. **Keep your opinion to yourself, you are not in charge.**

If the other team are tackling you too hard, **pass the ball earlier** and get rid of it instead of holding it too long. Don't give them a chance to get near you.

In every single case you have the power to deal with the issue in front of you.

Stan Jordan has eight self mentoring questions that he suggests you ask yourself every day and the 6th one is relevant to this situation and has had a profound effect on the way I interact with difficult team members.

Who Is Really In Charge?

If you indulge in blame and justification are you really in charge?

Absolutely not! You are handing over control to someone or something else.

I had a very personal experience of this myself this season. I play in a team as well and in many ways I was experiencing the total opposite in my over 45's team to what we were experiencing in the under 16's team.

We have a player in our team who seems to delight in telling me what I'm doing wrong. How I should have placed the ball or whether he feels I'm offside or whether I should have lifted my head more or any number of other infringements he feels I did wrong.

I've had this experience over many years and this season it was getting too much. In one particular game it did get too much and the dam burst. I lost my lolly.

That's about as polite as I can be when describing the scene because it was quite a tantrum on my behalf.

I felt drained, exhausted and then he was on my back even more throughout the game making sure to point out every mistake I made, of which I made many due to the emotional exhaustion I felt.

If only he would shut up, if only he wasn't on my team. If only..... there's the clue. I was below the line. But how could that be? It wasn't me making the comments and pulling down my team mates, It wasn't me....

Hold on. Stan's 6th mentoring question kicked in here. Who was really in charge? Clearly not me. And if I'm not in charge then I'm not playing above the line.

Shit! I really wanted to have someone tell me it was all his fault, I was right and it was totally out of line for him to make the kinds of comments he does.

If that was the case then the only power to deal with it lay in someone else's hands. Not mine and if there was one thing I believe to be true in every situation is that I have the choice of how to react, and I have the power.

Who was really in control that day? He was...Not me!

People will do all sorts of things to achieve significance, get attention and be reminded that they are important. And by offering these "helpful suggestions" it gave him a feeling of significance. It's the same mechanism for the young attention seekers in the U/16's.

When they wind someone up to the point of explosion then they are in control. Look what I can do! I can get you so wound up that you lose your lolly. Then I get to feel superior. And significant.

What can I do about it?

Just observe it dispassionately was the recommendation from Stan. So I took what's called the meta position. The position of the observer while still a participant in the interaction.

The Meta position is a psychological term that describes the clinician being able to partake in the interaction but also observe the overall meaning, motives and sub-context of the conversation form a third position. Like when you are watching two people in a heated discussion and you can see another level to the conversation without being involved or emotionally attached to the outcome.

As I observed the interactions of this player in subsequent weeks I noticed that he did the same thing to others as well. And a few weeks later he pushed another of our players, with a volley of helpful observations about what he should have done, to the point that he was going to thump him.

It's not about me at all. It's not that he thinks I'm a crap player and need a vast amount of instruction or that I don't know what I'm doing. It's not about me in any way. I'm just the bunny that he gets a rise out of…or at least one of them now.

With that knowledge I found the rest of my season far less stressful. And I'm so thankful for that opportunity to learn to see things from a different perspective.

He still tells me what I'm doing wrong, actually he tells everyone what they are doing wrong. But I just don't care. I'm back in control of my game.

I found this insight helpful when dealing with my U/16's too. The noisy ones, the ones that think they know it all are really just looking for significance. Which I can't give them. No one can give them that. It's something you need to give yourself. So If you engage in it you are only pouring water into a bucket with many

Playing above the line

holes. It will never fill up.

My job is to remind them that they agreed to play above the line and hope that the results they were seeing would be correctly attributed to that.

What does above the line sound like on the soccer pitch?

Our goal keeper begged for a run on the field. Like all goal keepers, in my experience, they feel they make great strikers too.

So we put him in for a half to show us what he's got. He missed a few sitters right in front of goal and one of our team, Harry, shouts out some derisive comments to him. Like he really needed to feel worse for missing the shot.

I shouted to the players *"Oi, Above the line please"*.

He thinks for a second, looks toward his team mates and replies *"Nice effort Mat, better luck next time"*.

And it's as simple as that.

And within a few short minutes Mat had indeed scored a brace of goals..

In every team I have taught this to, the phrase "that's below the line" has become a significant part of the team language.

It turns out that this is a great way to take a complex idea like; we all agreed to behave a certain way in this situation and right now you are not living up to your end of the bargain, it's letting the entire team down and your performance isn't very good either so, what are we going to do about that? And turn it into a positive way to keep the team working without getting dragged down into personal attacks. It seems to keep the personal judgments out of it and seems to help the individual within the team to take account of whether or not they are engaging in behaviours that are just not helpful to the mission.

This is what happened in our team because every player at some point in the season called someone on playing below the line. And they still managed to work remarkably together. No hurt feelings, no wounded pride, just honest assessment correction and get on with it.

Correction Without Invalidation

Correction without invalidation is a concept that my Mentor Stan Jordan also taught me. He directed me to a poem by Stewart Emery. There are so many foundational ideas for success in this one verse that it warrants reading a number of times. It is a principal that I have used over and over with the Saints team and with my business clients.

Mastery By Stewart Emery

Mastery in our careers (and in our lives!) requires that we constantly produce results beyond and out of the ordinary.

Mastery is a product of consistently going beyond our limits.

For most people, it starts with technical excellence in a chosen field and a commitment to that excellence. If you're willing to commit yourself to excellence, to surround yourself with things that represent this excellence, your life will change.

It's remarkable how much mediocrity we live with, surrounding ourselves with daily reminders that average is somehow acceptable.

In fact, our world suffers from terminal normality.

Take a moment to assess all the things around you that promote your being "average."

These are the things that prevent you from going beyond the limits that you've arbitrarily set for yourself.

The first step to mastery is the removal of everything in your environment that represents mediocrity, and one way to attain that objective is to surround yourself with people who ask more of you than you would ordinarily give of yourself. Didn't your parents and some of your best teachers and coaches do exactly that?

Another step on the path to mastery is the removal of resentment toward the master. Develop compassion for yourself so that you can be in the presence of a master and grow from the experience.

Rather than comparing yourself to (and resenting) people who have mastery, remain open and receptive. Let the experience be like the planting of a seed within you that, with nourishment, will grow into your own individual mastery.

You see, we're all ordinary. But rather than condemning himself for his "ordinariness," a master will embrace that ordinariness as a foundation for building the extraordinary.

Rather than relying on his ordinariness as an excuse for inactivity, he'll use it instead as a vehicle for correcting himself.

It's necessary to be able to correct yourself without invalidating or condemning yourself to use the results of the correction process to improve upon other aspects of your life. <u>Correction is essential to power and mastery</u>.

Smart successful people seem to talk less, listen more and always assume there is something more to learn about a topic, even if they are experts in that area.

In fact, the less successful people that I know have a lot to say about everything. They assume they know and that their opinions are correct and they won't shut up about it.

The problem with this is that they shut down the possibility of an alternative perspective or new way of thinking for any given situation and they remain just where they are in their development, they never evolve.

500 Years ago this kind of thinking is where most of the world was at with a very firm belief that the world was flat, and if you sailed off too far you would simply fall off the end into oblivion. So strong was this belief that laws were passed and lives were at stake if you had an alternative point of view.

This same 500 year old style of thinking pervades our work places, our teams and our lives. It is no longer a useful or resourceful way of thinking in our world yet I see so many people give into it.

What this sounds like, is when one of my team says, with total conviction, that we should play this formation because their favourite team plays that way, or this guy should be up front because he simply runs fast, or it's o.k. to play a no look pass because it worked this one time and they'll get quite argumentative about defending the position, quite confrontational.

What it sounds like in a work place is…. We've tried that and it doesn't work. We had an incentives program and it was a disaster, we're not going there again, direct marketing doesn't work anymore, etc.

What's common with this approach is that it closes off your mind to the other possibilities to solve a problem.

500 Year Old Thinking

If Christopher Columbus had not challenged the thinking of his time and sallied off beyond where they believed the edge of the world was then our earth would have remained closeted in very small thinking.

How many times have you seen a teenager cross their arms, roll their eyes and mentally check out. I've seen it a lot. Those players will not evolve very far until they open themselves up to the possibility of alternatives and to the possibility of Correction without invalidation.

What this means to me is that correction is required, constantly required, for mastery over a given task and that correction means that you don't discount, discredit or invalidate all the learning and activity that came before. Learning and mastery over a task is a constant evolution and if we assign valued based language to the efforts that you've made along the way then you are invalidating the experience and the process of mastery.

Right now I'm learning to Kite-Surf and it's quite a process of learning. Every minute that I'm engaged is a learning experience and what was nearly impossible to me a few weeks ago is slowly becoming manageable as I get more experience. If we were to suggest that everything I did up to date was wrong and invalidate the experience then I would be in a constant search for the one way that is right, the one solution that would make everything click together. It would also leave me constantly perplexed and slightly paranoid about all the wrong advice I had been given.

It sounds preposterous when I'm talking about an activity like kite-surfing. We all recognise that we start with baby steps, learning the basics, getting good at those before advancing to the next level. Advice and information we receive from instructors is not right or wrong, it's just information that I'll use at the right time.

I search out a multitude of experience and information from a variety of different sources and rather than condemning myself to the results of my first pitiful attempts to kite-surf, I begin to embrace the ordinariness and the corrections required to master the skill. I use the results of the correction process to improve and achieve mastery and eventually power over this very challenging activity. Soon it will become 2nd nature.

It confounds me that so many people invalidate the process of mastery in the search of new skills within our teams. They dismiss the results of the correction process and invalidate the process of mastery.

I see this in our Saints team and have decided to make it simple for them to understand when they are below the line on this particular process.

Anytime you put the word "but" in front of something you are about to say you are effectively invalidating the experience that comes before it. And that puts you right below the line. You'll end up, very quickly, in blame and Justification, and most likely an unrealistic appraisal about the possible corrections and outcomes.

Two things that will help you out here.
1. Replace the word "but" with "and." It will open your mind to other possibilities and corrections on your way to mastery.

2. Rather than take the arms folded stance when seeking out solutions, replace that 500 year old black and white thinking with a more evolutionary approach. Observations, inquisitiveness and openness. It was this kind of thinking that led to the greatest discoveries for mankind, from Darwin to Plato, from Zukkerberg to Columbus.

The only laws I'm not willing to challenge are the laws of physics.
A useful approach that I particularly like is the one that Amazon boss Jeff Bezos uses. He says that the only laws he is not willing to challenge are the laws of physics, other than that everything is up for grabs.

I have never met him but I imagine he doesn't use the 500 year old black and white, right or wrong thinking when he is looking for how Amazon.com can evolve. I imagine that he is inquisitive and investigates a particular perspective, using the alternative thinking to challenge his own current processes and test if a new correction might be resourceful for the evolution of his business.

The result is that Amazon is on it's way to becoming the first trillion dollar company and is one of the most successful business enterprises of our generation.

The smartest, most successful people in the world embrace correction without invalidation in their businesses and their lives. They embrace lifelong learning and accept evolutionary thinking as a part of their mastery. So why shouldn't we take that approach as well?

If we accept that the only laws that are set in stone are the laws of physics, it opens us up to a multitude of options, solutions and corrections to get us where we would love to be.

Playing above the line

If we engage in 500 year old, black and white thinking we are destined to remain with the multitude of people who are convinced they know and are destined to repeat the same mistakes over and over.

This is a fairly big step for a group of teenage soccer players to take on. A mindset of openness is one that needs to be vigorously defended at nearly every training. Each pronouncement, rather than being put down, needs to be explored.

In a typical pronouncement on the side line at half time, someone would make a suggestion of moving players around. *"We need to put Cody up at striker"* Someone would say. Rather than shut ourselves off to that thinking, I'd ask "*O.K. tell me how you'd re arrange the team to maintain the structure if we went down that path?"* . Typically what would happen is that the plan hadn't been thought through that far. *"I don't know I just think we need some pace up the front"* was the reply. If we did go that road we could possibly play this person in that position…and on we'd go for a few minutes exploring how we could make that work. We'd explore what that option would look like and eventually we decided that the structure was fine just how we had it. Other times we did change things around to accommodate a particular circumstance and it was brilliant, but it always came about from looking at the whole picture, not just one part of the story.

I know many sports coaches who spend entire seasons just coaching their strikers, I suppose in the belief that if they just concentrate on them and score more goals, that will be all they need to win. But looking at the whole picture is essential to finding a balance in your team and, I believe, developing a winning team. It certainly was in our experiment.

So encouraging the guys and gal in our team to use evolutionary thought was a cornerstone of my approach. As always, using questions to illicit a deeper thought process was far more effective than simply lecturing to them.

Staying Above The Line Myself
One of the best ways I've found to stay above the line is with a series of self mentoring questions, usually asked daily, that Stan

has taught me.

Going through this checklist will help you determine if you are playing above or below the line.

Self Mentoring questions that were passed onto me by Stan Jordan's.

1. What am I doing today to get what I want? Am I majoring in minors or giving the right attention to the majors?
2. Will my actions improve my situation and move me to where I want or am I settling?
3. How would the person I want to become do the things I am about to do?
4. How long can I hold my vision? (being clear on your why) e.g. 20 reasons why I'm a [your job] soccer coach to this team.
5. Am I willing to accept the consequences of not changing?
6. WHO IS IN CONTROL?, e.g. Am I being led by someone else or am I in control of myself?
7. What don't I see?
8. Am I setting in motion the causes that will produce the effect I want?

Playing above the line

CHAPTER 7.
THE SEASON SO FAR; PRACTICE THE WAY YOU INTEND TO PLAY

During pre-season one of the best results I thought we achieved was to eliminate blame and excuses from our vocabulary. We learnt how to keep each other accountable without getting personal or attacking each other.

It's amazing how the knock on effect of understanding above and below the line had on these kids lives. I have heard through the grapevine that they've started using this language in their lives outside our team. More than one parent has heard the expression, "that's below the line" and needed an explanation. At School too, I had heard stories of one of the team keeping his or her team mate above the line in their schoolwork.

If someone did go down that route, it began with me saying that's below the line, but in a very short period the rest of the team picked up the mantle and were calling each other on it as well. They especially enjoyed calling me on it when I occasionally slipped below the line.

We kicked off the season not quite knowing what effect it would have on results.

The first game we won 3:0 and the interplay between all areas of the team were very positive.

I even had some of the parents measure how long we played in our half and their half. I wanted data on their performance to see where we could improve. Professional athletes have game stats on how many completed passes they make, how many shots on goal they made or how many tackles they won. I figured if we didn't measure it we couldn't manage it. If you've ever had a business coach worth their salt you would have heard that one thrown at you.

The 2nd game we also won, and the third and fourth. I was seeing a transformation right before my eyes. I saw players giving absolutely everything, nearly to the point of having to crawl off the field. I saw team play and communication like I'd never seen with this bunch of people. And I saw it come together in the heat of battle.

They would muck around at training and at warm up, having quite a laugh. My assistant coach would sometimes have a go at them to smarten up. But come game day all the training we'd done in how to function as a team, who was responsible for what came together. It seemed to be that the pressure of the game, the furnace of the competition is where it all came together.

I had read about this quality in teams In some of the literature. Blair Singer, whose work I admire enormously, says that he has never seen a team come together unless their feet were held to the fire. Unless the team comes under pressure to have to come together and work toward the mission while under pressure.

And that's what seemed to be happening here. Under the pressure of game day they were really coming together and they were performing as a winning team.

No More Marquee Player
On week 4 we had a real test. One of our attacking midfielders who was fast and assertive on the field was leaving for a family holiday for 5 weeks. There was a sense of "oh no, now this

winning streak will come to an end." But that didn't happen at all.

We continued to win game after game. We were coming up against the same teams we played last year who beat us and we had them totally under control.

In the 5 weeks that our winger was away, we didn't drop a single game. Some of his close buddies were quite vocal about the result his absence would have on the results, but they were proved wrong.

What that did was instill a belief in the remaining players that we weren't reliant on any 1 particular player. We weren't in trouble if one of our "marquee' players couldn't make a game. The entire team could in fact come together and use their code of honour to make sure that we continued to post result after result.

There is an unusual thing that happens in a game right after a team scores. If you've ever watched any team sport you will have seen it. The team that scores suddenly becomes invincible for the next 5 minutes. Their energy level increases, their commitment to challenges goes through the roof, their exhaustion seems to fade and their tails are up. They will often score another goal quite quickly because of this apparent boost in their game.

If you are defending against this it is the most dangerous time because the opposition seem to be doing everything right for a time and just can't put a foot wrong.

This is the effect the wins were having on us as a team. We were seeing gradual progress, small wins that became bigger wins, always progressing. It gave us this incredible lift in our performance.

Practice The Way We Intend To Play
Practice the way we intend to play – our training must have the same mindset as we want to use on the game day. If we muck around and practice the wrong thing at training then we will use the wrong thing on game day.

This is a principal of coaching and is often very difficult to maintain with a bunch of teenagers who are pumped to the eyeballs with the natural hormones of early adolescence.

I want the trainings to be fun but focused and sometimes it was difficult to maintain that focus. They wanted it to err on the side of fun a little too much at times.

But it's a dangerous principal to ignore, bad habits creep in if you rehearse them over and over and as any smoker will tell you, its much harder to give up once you've started. So I opt for not getting addicted to bad habits in the first place.

Perhaps the best explanation for this came from a professional musician friend of mine. He is a band coach and helps amateur bands get their act together so they can gig and perform professionally.

He points out that bands and individual players will often learn a part in a song incorrectly, perhaps a few notes variation, or they start at the wrong place or on the wrong beat, and from that point everything is slightly out of time and not quite right. But they practice this way over and over again without ever getting it just right. The result is that the whole band doesn't quite perform that piece as well as it could have.

The problem is right back at the beginning. They have learnt the piece incorrectly in the first place, and by repeating it over and over it has become correct in their own mind or their version of correct. That inaccurate translation becomes the new norm. And I can't tell you how fiercely they'll defend that version until you break down the original song and show them note for note, beat by beat how they have altered the original version.

By repeating the wrong thing over and over it will appear to be the right thing.

The more you practice it the more entrenched that version of the song will become until eventually it will be very difficult to convince you otherwise.

I see this on the soccer field with players doing stuff on the practice pitch that they think is cool or fun, mostly in an attempt to get attention, that I wouldn't accept on the soccer field.

I see that in businesses as well. People talk to each other in a way that is unacceptable behind closed doors and then they naively think that wont translate to their customers. What you practice every day will become your new norm. No matter if it is right or wrong.

There are so many ramifications for this knowledge.

But one that I feel is particularly important is mental rehearsal.

What you practice in your mind becomes your reality, so choose what you practice wisely.

I read of a study some time ago of a basketball coach who did an experiment to test mental rehearsal. He took 3 groups of players.

One group practiced shooting baskets manually for 5 weeks, physically shooting baskets for hours each day.

Another group did mental rehearsal every day, spending some time going through the actions in their mind about improving their shooting and putting that ball in the hoop.

The third group were the control group and did no practice or rehearsal at all.

The results after 5 weeks:
Not surprisingly, the group that did no practice showed no improvement, in fact their performance went a little backwards.

Playing above the line

The group that did the physical practice improved by about 15%. Not a bad result.

The group that only did mental rehearsal improved by around 23%. They had not laid hands on a basketball for 5 weeks yet their shooting accuracy improved by a massive 23%.

So working on your mental game appears to have more impact than working on your physical game.

That doesn't mean I'm not going to work with both.

One evening after we had been playing for about 7 games I noticed a few of the boys starting to get really cocky and over confident. They were doing what I call no-look passes and making decisions in the training that I absolutely would not like to see in a soccer game.

I offered the idea that I wanted us to train the way we intend to play and all hell broke loose.

I had quite an upset on my hands and I was in the middle of a few fired up team members who had started "practicing the song" (or in this case, the way they passed the ball) incorrectly in the first place and their particular version of the "song" had become entrenched in their mind as the right way. In this case they were practicing a trick they had seen on television many times, the no look pass.

A no-look pass is when you get totally closed down and so you either hit the ball with your back heel without sighting the team mate you are passing to, or you anticipate where you think someone will be and knock it to them without looking. A good defensive team will recapture that ball very quickly and probably hit you with a counter attack while your no look passer is still scratching their head wondering what just happened.

Because they are young and athletic and full of bravado, three of the team members were adamant that they could pull this off and were extremely forceful about their defense of this type of play.

The best way to deal with being closed down on the side line, in my opinion, is to find one of your team mates who is facing the right way and complete a pass to them that has the highest chance of being received. The defenders will then flock to the ball and you will be standing free to receive the ball back from your team mate without any pressure. It's a classic version of going backwards and is often the first step to moving forward.

It also fits my principal of play the ball the way you are facing, because the pass completion has a high chance of success. A no-look pass forward on the other had has a very low chance of remaining in our possession. We lose control very quickly when plays like this are made. It's a "Hail Mary" option and I'm not prepared to play that way until there is absolutely no other option available. In my teams, there is always another option because one of your team mates always has your back and is ready to support you.

This was the setting for quite an upset on this particular training night.

There were words said and tempers flared and after quite a lot of evidence was presented to them they still were not prepared to back down. The training was thrown into chaos and I decided to call it off early. I was upset and continuing on would have only put ingredients into play that would lead somewhere very unproductive.

Here is the email I sent the next day.

Hi guys

A few things about training tonight.

While I want you all to really enjoy yourselves at training and have fun, it's a learning environment and my job is to teach you to be a high performing team and improve your soccer skills while we are at it. So far it's been working very well and our results to date show that.

When you either say to your self....Yeah I know that, or argue with me, or try to prove me wrong, what you are actually doing is shutting yourself off from learning.

When you shut yourself off from learning, then your skills and ability stop dead in their tracks.

I know you are all at an age where you have a tendency to believe you know everything, however if your team and soccer skills stay at this level then you are missing out on so much. And shutting yourselves off from a world of opportunities.

If you are open to replacing "I know" or the urge to "prove me wrong" with the phrase "that's interesting" then your brain will switch on to learning new things that might improve not only your soccer game but how you work within a high performing team.

The reason I want you to play a 2 touch passing game is to improve your decision making ability before you get the ball. You only have 1 touch to control it and another touch to send it. So the shape of your body before you receive the ball is critical, and what you do with the 1st touch is vital. Otherwise you'll find yourself stuck with no other options than to make a pass that has less than 10% chance of getting to your team mate.

The reason I asked you not to make trick passes or to make back heel no-look passes is this...... I want us to train the way we intend to play on Saturday.

I believe that if you fool around at training and spend a lot of time practicing unsighted passes and unnecessary trick passes then you have taught your body and brain to use those and you can't help but end up using them in a game. It is not possible to say, yeah but I wont use it in a game.

What you practice over and over again is what you will end up doing and if you practice a poor technique, poor decision making or poor discipline, then that's what shows in your game.

I called off training early last night because it wasn't working for me. And I wasn't prepared to compromise on what I believe is important.

A number of players were intent on proving me wrong and were

unwilling to let it go. This totally shut down the learning for the entire team. I attempted to get back to game play a number of times but the behaviour and attitude of a number of players made this an impossible task.
So I called it off.

Yes I was upset, and frustrated because, for some of you, rather than opening yourselves to learning you just wanted to do what you already knew and were disrespectful of me and the remainder of the team in how you went about it.

No team comes together without standing in the heat of conflict and staying with it to work it out. And no team comes together without having a strong code of honour.

Moving forward are you willing to agree to…

- *Replace "I know" with "that's interesting".*
- *Train how we intend to play. With fun and focus.*
- *Speak supportively and respect different viewpoints.*
- *Focus on what works.*
- *Play above the line. Take responsibility for your contribution and performance.*
- *Be responsible for yourself - Do not lay blame or justify. Be responsible for your own production, attitude and contribution to the team.*

See you on Saturday.

We went on the following Saturday to win 3:0 and they played with integrity. A few players came up and apologized for the way they behaved at training and acknowledged that they were out of line. I thought that was huge for testosterone fuelled young men and I had even more respect for them for doing that.

No team comes together unless they learn to stand in the heat of conflict, and that's exactly what we had just done.

Playing above the line

CHAPTER 8.
CREATING A SET OF RULES TO GOVEREN
OUR BEHAVIOUR - OUR CODE OF HONOUR

How do you get a group of people who have come together to achieve a task to behave in a way that allows them to perform and flourish?

You create a code of honour to govern the internal behaviours of the team and you do this by creating and agreeing to a set of rules.

It's not unlike the games we played as children.

We set up the game and agree on what actions would win the game. We agreed on what was out of bounds, what was B.A.R. (that's the safe place where you couldn't be caught) and what the rules were. I don't know about you but the rules were debated a little before everyone agreed on them and the game began in earnest.

If you didn't play by the rules then the first call was "cheater" and typically someone would appeal to the others in the group, often accompanied by a finger pointing at the transgressor… "He was cheating, that's not fair!" If it was resolved then the game went on. If not the game broke down and everyone went their own way.

I was profoundly influenced by author Blair Singer and his book "Team Code of Honour".

In it he outlines the extreme importance of having a code of honour to govern the internal behaviour of the team. Without it you will not have a functioning team because what you will get is a group of people all playing by different rules.

Everyone has a set of rules of the game that they live and work by, and those rules are influenced by many, many things. The culture of the family you grew up in, your experience in previous teams, your peers and mentors you admire and your personal disciplines.

Let me give you an example; What rules of the game to you set for yourself when keeping time agreements? Do you see the time you agreed to meet someone as set in stone and sacrosanct? Or do you see it as a rough guide only.

I am a little pedantic about meeting times. I think that if you are on time then you are actually a little late. If you are 5 minutes early then that's on time. If I've agreed to meet you at 3pm then I prepare to leave to make the meeting with more than enough time for things to go wrong and still be on time, even with heavy traffic, an unknown location, forgetting my wallet, etc. I move heaven and earth to be where I said I'd be when I said I'd be there. And if something totally unforeseen goes wrong then you'll hear from me prior to the meeting. It might be a text 10 minutes before our agreed meeting time letting you know that I'm running 5 minutes late.

Others don't have the same approach to meeting times. I have many friends and family who just don't approach it the same way. My sister is so predictably bad at keeping meeting times that we now tell her we are meeting about 30 minutes prior to when we actually meet. We have close friends that don't adhere to time rules at all and move to deal with whatever crisis is in front of them without much preparation or concern for how that might affect the schedule of the day or the agreed meeting times with others.

Neither approach is right or wrong. There is no absolute correctness, only a reaction to each choice. What I learnt in science could easily be applied here, for every action there is an equal and opposite reaction. For every choice on how to manage your time for example, there is a reaction and consequence. For me the consequence is that I'm considered reliable and I can manage lots of tight appointment times in my work day, but the downside is that I'm often unnecessarily stressed out about being 3 minutes late for a meeting.

If neither is right or wrong then why do such differences cause great upsets within groups?

It is simply that we haven't agreed on the rules of our game we are about to play. In this case it's the game of how do we manage our time together. I'm playing by one set of rules and you may or may not be playing from another set of rules and no one knows when someone is playing by the rules or not.

The result of this is that we start to keep score in an unproductive way. If one member of the team is consistently late to training and everyone else is on time, then the on time members start to keep a score. If the coach doesn't pull them up on that or there are no rules of the game around this then resentment builds.

Every time it happens the score keeps climbing and the resentment builds. The team members are asking themselves why the coach doesn't pick this up and they are starting to say "that's not fair". They typically don't point the finger like we did in those childhood games but rest assured they are feeling the same emotions they felt when they were finger pointing.

Eventually the score gets too high and they start to think to themselves, *"well if it's o.k. for him to be late then I'm going to be late too"*. And then you have a breakdown in the teams code of honour.

If you don't create a set the rules for the game that govern your internal behaviours then you are at the mercy of each team members own set of rules of the game. And they are very rarely homogeneous.

Playing above the line

With my bunch of teenagers I had a very wide set of rules of the game. Some were very similar and others massively different. In all areas of team behaviour. Time management, trainings, attitude, approach to authority, commitment, agreements, you name it we had a wide variety of views.

And of course being the age they were, each and everyone of them firmly believed their approach to be the best and only way to do things. The conviction and certainty of youth is an interesting thing to handle and it's something I needed to manage every week. I am often reminded of the phrase "they don't even know how much they don't know" and it comforts me when I'm facing a raging teenager totally convinced that his no-look pass is the best way to handle a tight situation on the field when every adult on the field is telling them it's not.

We needed a set of rules to help me lead the team and let them know what's expected of them, and to give us all clear boundaries to let each other know when we were out of line with the rules.

Following are the rules that we used;

1. Have a willingness to win and let other team members win.

2. When something is not working, first look to how you can contribute to fixing it. Don't attack or blame your team mates

3. Commit 100% to your team, training and game day. If you can't give 100% on the field then sub yourself off for a rest.

4. Only make agreements you intend to keep. Communicate and clear up any potential broken agreements at the first opportunity.

5. Every team member is responsible for continuing to improve the team.

6. Celebrate and acknowledge that the entire team contributes to a winning performance, not just the one who puts the ball into the net. Find awesome ways to celebrate (e.g. team go-cart days).

7. Focus on what works and propose solutions and ideas at the pre game warm up and at half time. We won't make fun of any idea.

8. Respect the refs decision, even if you don't agree with it. When in doubt or when you feel angry at a decision or an opposition players' treatment of you...take a break to avoid retaliation.

9. Play with heart and play for your team mates. That means we never give up or give in until the whistle has been blown.

10. Support risk taking by team members. If you see them making a great move, ask yourself "how can I support that move?".

11. We will play above the line. Take ownership, be accountable to our team mates and take responsibility for our actions.

Calling It: how to deal with breaches of the rules without causing undue conflict.

Whenever I talk about rules of the game peoples thoughts turn fairly quickly to what happens when it goes wrong. How do I deal with telling my team mate that they aren't doing what they agreed to do.

If you are a 'High I' like me, then confronting transgressions are not a natural thing to do. If you are a 'High C' or 'High D' and you are quite task oriented then you'll likely have no problem confronting this. But there will likely be some hurt feelings and upsets along the way.

What we really need is a way to call each other on it without it being a big deal or a personal attack.

That's where debriefing comes in.
But before I get into that, I want to say that the combination of a

few things comes into play here.

Managing by agreement, playing above the line and the massive increase in trust that this approach has seems to create an environment that is non combative, for the most part, and seems to be conducive to holding each other accountable.

There seems to be a different neural pathway that these requests take in the brain of someone who is asked rather than told. Someone who has had a strong hand in choosing the goal and creating the rules of the game. The team begins to police themselves and individuals accept a greater level of self discipline.

I even use it at home to great effect.

If any of you have teenage children then you'll know how difficult it is to get them to do the chores. It's a constant frustration of asking that the chores be done and then coming back later to discover that something has distracted them, usually a computer game or a Skype call with friends, and the chores remain undone. The explanation of why they weren't done just doesn't stack up and frustration and anger build between both parties.

So I thought I'd try managing by agreement at home. It sounds like this.

"Loch, it's your turn to clean up the kitchen tonight, are you ok to get that finished before bed time?"

"Yes dad." At this point you know that it hasn't registered.

So I try a different approach.

"Loch. You know how we agreed that everyone has to do some chores to contribute to the household?"

"Yes dad"

"And you agreed that you would do your fair share."

"Yes"

"Tonight it's your turn to clean up the kitchen after dinner, Are you willing to get that done before you go to bed?"

"Yes"

"Are you absolutely sure? Because if there is something genuine that is more important or urgent now is the time to tell me about it."

"I said yes" with accompanied eye rolling.

99% of the time it gets done, even if I can hear him doing the dishes late at night because he got tied up in a game and forgot until he went to go to bed.

And if it doesn't get done it sounds like this.

"Loch, you agreed to clean up the kitchen last night and I see it hasn't happened, what's up with that?"

Insert excuse here, which he knows is not going to help in any way and he gives up fairly quickly.

"Well you agreed to do it, you made an agreement with me last night and I expect you to keep your agreements, so can you get it done now?

" I suppose"

It sure beats ranting and raving at them about doing their chores.

And that's how you keep your team mates playing above the line as well.

Ask For Their Agreement
Double check that there are no hurdles to getting a task done. If there are, deal with them up front.
Then let them get on with it.

If they are outside the rules of the game then simply ask what's going on there? Remind them that they agreed to it and expect it to get fixed.

Debriefing

This is a really critical step for any team that wants to perform to a higher level.

One of the principals of good management is to be candid and honest about what is working and what is not working. But to do this in a way that helps rather than hinders is the real magic of debriefing. In His book "Winning" by Jack Welsh it is the willingness to be candid and honest with people that he credits as being one of the key factors to his position as a world leader in management.

We've all known coaches, players and managers who screamed, yelled, bullied and dragged a performance out of their team. I've known of hugely famous football players and coaches who are known for this approach. Our experience with Coach X earlier in the season was just such a case in point.

But I don't believe this provides the best learning opportunity for a team member to improve. Wanting to avoid the pain of a verbal barrage from an angry team mate is one level of motivation. But I believe it breeds resentment, anger, destroys cohesion and it certainly obliterates the opportunity to learn from your mistakes.

Every mistake is an opportunity to learn

I believe that every mistake is an opportunity to learn. An opportunity to go to bed a little wiser than you woke up.

Here is how we debrief in our team;

What happened?

In this question we only want the facts…not the opinions. Example: The other team just scored a goal. Fred was late for training again.

Why did this happen?

This discussion must be kept brief and opinion free if possible.

This is the second most critical step:

A) *What worked or is working?**
B) *What is not working?*

Notice the language. It is not right or wrong... it either works or it does not. You have to find both. They always co-exist.

The most critical question:

What did you/we LEARN? And what are we going to do to correct it?

In this step you are looking for a PATTERN of behaviour or results... NOT a single isolated incident.

Examples: The last three goals were scored by the same guy from the same side of the field.

What can we do to correct or improve?

This question cannot be asked until the previous one is asked & answered. Otherwise you may put something into action that may create more problems than you had to begin with.

This whole sequence can take seconds, minutes or hours. I recommend minutes. Once this becomes a ritual, it will force accountability, quick correction and it will leave the emotion out of the process.

This sequence is the perfect format for team meetings, for time-outs, for questioning behaviour that is not in-line with the Code. Most importantly, it is what you must train the "little voice" in your brain to do any time there is a setback for yourself personally. This will keep you from taking it personally.

The Half Time Chat. Using The Debrief.

This was a really critical part of my game day strategy.
In previous years I had told the team what they were doing wrong and what I wanted them to improve, sometimes it worked, often

Playing above the line

not so much.

This year I decided to use a coaching technique that I find extremely helpful in by Business Coaching practice, especially when things aren't going so well.

I'd ask 2 questions and allow them to answer.

In most cases, once they feel they've discovered the problem it's highly likely that they already know the answer. The result is that without me telling them what they were doing wrong, they now know and they are also highly committed to the fix because they feel they came up with the idea. It's the ultimate persuasion. Leading them to discover the answer to the problem.

The 2 questions;

1. What are we doing best?
2. And what could we be doing better?*

Immediately, several team members would pitch in with some thoughts and my job was to lead the discussion. Occasionally I'd ask questions to reveal a bit more depth about whether this really was the area we needed to improve, or whether the solution they jumped to might have an adverse effect somewhere else on the field. But it was mostly questions and encouragement.

When it wasn't working so well the thing that was always said is that our communication needed to be better. And when we were on fire, the thing that was always said was that we were communicating better than the opposition. Interesting, isn't it?

The second thing that was often said is that the other team were playing below the line and we kept ourselves above the line. In the case of our Grand Final, my team commented that the opposition were so far below the line they were on the next page. They were full of blame and excuses and they just weren't sure how to fix it. Apparently the opposition sideline joined in below the line and my guys commented on that as well, not complaining just noticing.

I did see many of our players posses an inner confidence in themselves and their team mates that they weren't going to go there. They weren't going to descend to below the line. And what I particularly noticed was the effect it seemed to have on their physical performance. They seemed to run faster, the ball moved quicker up field and support was everywhere for any given option that we needed. The score line showed it as well. We won the Grand Final 5:1, only conceding when one of my very over confident and mouthy players got a little too cute and made a mistake, which we were duly punished for.

Our opposition were extremely good, although the score line doesn't reflect how good they were. Last season they beat us every game, and they were justifiably 2nd in the competition. But playing above the line, holding each member accountable for what they'd agreed to, especially when the pressure was on, is the secret sauce that made this group the legendary team they were.

Debriefing and constant correction without invalidating the previous effort was a major piece of the puzzle that helped us also.

You could follow it up with "what aren't we seeing" but that's a bit complicated for a group of 15 year olds. Very helpful for senior management especially if your team are putting together a pitch or proposal.

Playing above the line

CHAPTER 9.
WHAT MAKES THE GAME WORTHWHILE MAINTAINING MOTIVATION

About 5 weeks into the season, after discovering that we were unbeaten to date I wondered if increasing the challenge might be a way to keep the team motivated.

So I posed the question. Do you think we should raise the stakes of our goal this season? Do you think we could get through the season and get to the Grand Final unbeaten? There was an immediate and spontaneous response, *"Hell yes! Lets do it!"* And I observed a huge increase in energy.

What I had done was set up a series of "flow experiences". This has come from the science of a very interesting guy who has discovered that happiness comes not just from a lack of stress and pressure, but from the opportunity to bring your skills to a challenge that is slightly beyond you but not too far out of reach. These are called a flow experience and the happiest people in the world, he discovered, had a regular series of these flow experiences.

Playing above the line

Mihaly Csikszentmihalyi grew up in Europe during the second world war. After it was all over he began to see the world around him in a different light, clearly he had a natural inquisitiveness that would help him become one of the worlds leading scientists, and one of the leaders in positive psychology in the decades to come. As a young child he realised so few of the grown-ups he knew were able to withstand the tragedies that the world visited on them.

He saw how few of them could take on a normal contented and happy life after the war. He became fascinated with what contributed to a life that was meaningful and satisfied. He wondered what contributed to happiness.

He worked with a musician who tells a story of writing music almost on auto pilot. For this he must have a high level of skill in his musicianship because if you or I entered this creative state without the necessary skill I don't think the notes would be so beautifully arranged. The immersion in the field of excellence you are engaged in must be significant, you must be highly skilled.

So many people described this experience as a spontaneous flow that he began to describe this altered state as a "flow experience".

Athletes and sports people who were part of the study often described this as being in the zone, that the conditions were such that everything clicked, everything felt good and easy.

He went on to measure, very accurately, the level of challenge and the level of skill people brought to a task and to discover how it affected their sense of flow.

The real question is, how can we put more and more of life into this flow channel? And in my little group, the question was how do I keep my team in a state of flow for as much of the time as is possible?

Why would I want to do that? Because the more flow experiences you have in your day the higher you would rate your happiness according to Csikszentmihalyi. One of the ways he suggests to move into the flow channel is to have a group of skilled players and increase the challenge level.

This is exactly what I decided to do. By increasing the challenge and the mission. Setting this new challenge meant that often players needed to step up and do things that were outside their normal skill zone. A great example of this was a game where we were a goal down and time was closing out. It was beginning to look like we would see our first defeat of the season. Juan, who was not one of the more skilled or experienced players clearly made a decision to make it happen when an opportunity arose.

The game had been very tight and we had been marked nearly out of the game. They knew who our star scorers were and they had them covered. Juan was not one of our usual scorers, although he puts away a few great goals each season. He received the ball in the attacking half and his usual move was to pass the ball off quite quickly, but today he saw a gap and ran with the ball. He managed to turn the first defender, beat the next one in a brilliant run toward the edge of the box. He was then confronted with the 2 central defenders who were about to shut down this nonsense when he let fly with a beautiful shot across them all and slotted the ball into the top corner of the goal to bring us level with only 4 minutes till the whistle.

That day he was held aloft by his team mates as his moment of brilliance saved our bacon and we continued on toward the mission of remaining undefeated. On that day Juan rose to a challenge that was a little beyond him and brought skills to the task that he'd been practicing for the last 2 years. If you asked him he'd say time seemed to stand still and he entered a different state of reality, for those few moments he was in a flow state and his skills and instincts took over as if automatically. He was able to bring those skills into play on the challenge in a nearly automatic state and he rounded those defenders in a way that was beyond his usual level.

Playing above the line

I'll bet he remembers this event often and I suspect that the memory of that contributes to his sense of happiness and wellbeing. We reminded him of it often throughout the season and every time he beamed with pride. He seemed to grow a few inches that day and I believe it was the result of creating and maintaining a challenge that was nearly beyond them, giving them the opportunity to enter the flow state as often as possible.

Encouraging Flow In Our Team

Because flow is linked closely with achievement, its development could have a positive effect in increasing satisfaction and accomplishment. Flow researchers, such as Csikszentmihalyi, believe that interventions may be useful to enhance and increase flow states in teams, through which people would gain 'intrinsic rewards that encourage persistence".

This certainly was what we experienced in our team. An increase in persistence and to a certain extent, resilience, was a great result of providing consistent challenges in an environment that was closely matched to the skill levels of our team mates. Often requiring a slight increase in the skill level to match the new challenge. Players were entering a flow state from both control and arousal state.

Your team will likely experience flow when they are doing their best work in a task that requires full involvement and focus and the skills for the task closely match ones ability.

Visser [21] in his book "Good Work" suggests that managers that want to increase levels of engagement, can provide tools by which you can create an atmosphere that makes it easier to enter flow states. This encourages greater levels of persistence in achieving tasks and happiness in your teams lives.

In order to achieve flow, Csikszentmihalyi says the following three conditions need to be present;

1. Clear goals

2. Immediate feedback
3. A balance between opportunity and capacity, or a balance between challenge and skills required

Flow is an innately positive experience and studies have shown that it produces feelings of enjoyment and sometimes feelings that are quite intense. These feelings are so intense that they contribute positively toward happiness in the long term. Some have suggested that continual small improvements and wins create a sense of meaning, achievement and satisfaction. In other words, happiness. The more you can engineer flow experiences into your teams work life the happier they will be, and the more motivated, focused and productive they'll be.

Attempting these new, difficult challenges of remaining unbeaten stretched our skills and the individuals emerged with great feelings of competence and mastery.

[21] Visser, Coert. "Good Business: Leadership, Flow, and the Making of Meaning". Retrieved 26 September 2012.

Playing above the line

CHAPTER 10.
TRANSITION - CHANGE IS CONSTANT

tran·si·tion   [tran-zish-uhn, -sish-] noun

Movement, passage, or change from one position, state,
stage, subject, concept, etc., to another; change:
e.g. the transition from adolescence to adulthood.

The single biggest element in winning a game is not how well the
striker scores or how brilliantly the defenders defend, or even the
pass completion rate of the midfielders. It's how players prepare
for and respond to the change of circumstances throughout the
game. Looking at the game from a different perspective, one can
say that any team sport is a game of constant change of
possession.

The Great Nevada Volleyball Competition

My team of three were by no means the best in this competition of
four beach volleyball teams. We weren't even the 2nd best. In fact,

Playing above the line

I'm fairly sure we were the weakest team in the competition, at least that's what the salivating stares from the other teams seemed to be saying to us. We were a group of business owners up at the crack of dawn, just as we had for the previous 9 days, duking it out on what passes for a beach volleyball court in a resort an hour outside Las Vegas. Effectively playing a game designed for the finest beaches in the world in the middle of the Nevada Desert.

Throughout the tournament the workshop leaders really messed with us, asking us to make tough decisions, awful decisions at times, with the end goal of winning this beach volleyball tournament. The winning team would take home the not insignificant pot of money that had been gathering as penalties for various transgressions throughout the 10 day course. Probably about $1000 US or so.

But more importantly than that was the steely competitive streak you will find in most business owners and leaders.

In our team we had a woman who was a former senior exec and to relax she flew planes and then skydived out of them with a dozen of her closest friends, but she hadn't touched a volleyball since collage. My other team mate was from Barbados, who was a hospitality genius and a lovely gentle man. And me the Aussie who was very at home on the beach but really the last time I played this game was when Mr Shipley, my year 10 PE teacher, made us play just to amuse himself.

We were not Olympic material, and the other teams knew it. They had some serious players, athletes and were extremely competitive by nature. They seemed to know tactics and could rattle off names of famous beach volleyball stars with the strategies they has used to win tournaments.

The could dig, set and spike that ball and they really ran us all over the court.

What I didn't know then was that they were a team of individual champions and they were keen to show off their champion skills. They even competed with each other to place the killer blow and finish off the competition, but this was mostly their downfall. This is how we found ourselves in the final for the competition.

The other teams, with individuals who had champion skills, kind of neutralised each other out and their games often ended in bickering, blame and excuses. But right now my team found ourselves in the final for this little tournament.

In the final game, complete with the other teams sitting on the side line watching us play and muttering to themselves, we gave it our best shot but quickly found ourselves down 7:2. They only had 4 more points and the tournament was done. We just couldn't match them for skill and they seemed to be really enjoying spiking that ball with all their might and taking another point from us.

Our team leader, Lisa called us together for a quick strategy session. Our team motto was never give up…ever. We knew that we didn't have the skills to wipe them off the floor so I offered up the idea of transition. The quicker we could move from our attack to a defensive position then we would be ready to handle anything they threw at us. So our strategy was just to get the ball back over as well as we could and then take up our positions on the court ready to return.

Whoever was nearest the ball would do whatever they could to get to the ball up in the air and back into play. We had the court covered as long as we could transition back to our starting positions. One of us would put it all on the line to get to that ball while the others dealt with getting it back over the net. Then as quickly as we could we'd be back ready for the next onslaught.

We threw ourselves back onto the fray but quickly saw the score go downhill and fairly soon we were looking at match point against us. 10:2. With our never give up attitude, pretty much all we had left in our arsenal was our team strategy which started to pay dividends at exactly the right time. We began to claw our way back. 10:3, then 10:4.

Every time we attacked we transitioned to defence immediately. The moment we finished our defence we transitioned to attack. We were getting it right over and over again, moving from one phase of play to another much quicker than the opposition.

They would try these huge smashing shots, and as they were about to congratulate themselves we'd return them, which they were not quite prepared for. They were not moving from attack to defence as smooth as we were. This increased their frustration and what happened next is something that I've seen countless times. They started to take an attitude of, if you want it done right you'll need to do it yourself. Which of course never seems to work out in a team game. They attempted more and more outrageous shots which really missed the mark. Their team mates started at them. *"What do you think you are doing?"* they argued. *"Well someone has to win this thing"* one of them replied. They started beating themselves up for missing shots they thought should have hit their mark, and then desperation started to set in as we started to draw closer and they couldn't get that final match point. At 10:8 they started getting really angry at each other. At 10:9 the desperation had well and truly turned to frustration. When we levelled at 10, we all suspected this might be the comeback of the century, in our little world at least.

What was happening on our side of the net was the total opposite. Fast transitions, individuals risking everything for their team mates, giving 100%. We were exhausted, our knees and hands were bleeding after diving for the ball in what passed for sand in the Nevada Desert resort. Our team talk was quiet and positive, encouraging and clear. We were not attempting anything flashy, just basics. Get the ball back every time and get ready for the next onslaught. I saw my other 2 team mates grow in stature, belief and determination as that game wore on.

We still had a mountain to climb because in order to win in beach volleyball we had to be clear by 2 points. So we battle on. They managed to take a point off us to get to 11:10 but we kept on with our strategy slowly getting closer, stronger and more resilient. We drew in front with the next few points and as we were serving for match point at 11:12 I looked around at the faces of my team mates and honestly I could have cried. I felt like we had been in battle together, we were on the brink of being slaughtered, only to stage a comeback of epic proportions, a genuine David versus Goliath battle. And right now I took a moment to look around. The opposition were beaten, they didn't have any fight left in them to rally a comeback, you could see it in the way they held themselves, full of recrimination, doubt and totally perplexed at what had just happened. Lisa, fittingly served the last ball and with what felt like an extra bolt of energy we took the last point off them to win the match.

It was a brilliant win orchestrated with outstanding leadership, using disciplined team principals we took on a stronger more talented opponent and won, with a huge comeback.

It was a feeling I'll never forget. I experienced a genuine closeness with my team, a camaraderie and a huge sense of achievement at what we had done. We began to refer to ourselves as team Lisa and I even heard others say they wished they had ended up on team Lisa. It's a closeness that still lasts to this day, many years later and across many continents.

I was feeling so proud and so full of energy. It is an experience that will stay with me forever. The win was born out of the simple principal of transition. Moving from one state to another quicker than the opposition. Being prepared to give 100% to our team mates to make sure we got the job done, and move from a defensive mindset to an offensive mindset in the blink of an eye.

Transition is a state of mind not just a technical phase of the game.

One of the areas I have been working on with the U/16's for the

Playing above the line

past few years was the transition phase of the game of Soccer. That is when you go from either attack to defence, or from defence to attack. The 2 principal requirements for this to be successful is the right mindset & preparation.

In football jargon you are only ever in one of three phases of play;

1. Possession of the Ball [PB]

2. Opposition to Possession of the ball [OP] or

3. Transition, either from possession to OP or vice versa.

In other words, if you are on the attack and you've committed players forward to support the move and suddenly play breaks down, you lose possession of the ball and you need to transition as quickly as you can to a defensive phase of play.

The aim of the game of soccer hasn't changed since it first began: Score more goals that the other guys and prevent the opposition from scoring against you. Sounds simple.

But soccer is a game of constant change of possession a constant movement of mindset.

So one team is always defending trying to win the ball, while the other wants to move the ball into scoring position and score. Unless the team in possession scores, there will be a change of possession. After the change of possession, everyone will need to transition to a different way of playing and thinking:

The team that lost the ball now needs to transition from attacking to defending, trying to force a turnover. The team that was defending now needs to transition to attacking. How best to do this?

The simple answer in today's soccer is:

AS FAST AS POSSIBLE

Speed is of the essence.

Transitioning to Defence;
You want your team to immediately pressure the ball and not let the opponent get organised into an attacking mode.

This requires mental and physical speed. Mentally, your players need to react extremely quickly to a change of possession, perceive the position and movement of their opponents and anticipate possible plays so they can prevent them.

Transitioning to Offense;
Your team has won possession of the ball. They should already anticipate what the opponent will do, i.e. Transition to defense and pressure the ball. Your goal is to get the ball moving towards the opponent's goal as quickly as possible, before the other team has done its job of marking and closing down options.

In this transition, your players also need to react quickly, perceive where the spaces and opponents movements are, anticipate plays and make the runs and passes quickly.

Why Is Transition So Important?
The concept of transition is all about how quickly you can change and adapt your behaviour from one state to another. And I believe it's ramifications are far greater than just the soccer pitch.

Every team has setbacks, it's just part of the game, but I believe that the quicker you can transition from a set back to a more resourceful mode of behaviour the quicker you will win the game.

And I'm not just talking about soccer. I'm talking about personal states, business, families, musicians, politicians… everyone.

Transition is a core belief of mine that has had great effect on the field and in business.

Just acknowledging that there will be a constant change of ball possession, or a constant change from attack to defence changes the way I think about teams.

I've learnt that games are a reflection of life. How we play a game is a direct reflection of how we deal with our lives and in many cases our businesses.

Why is it that sports people are so good at business? Look at legendary rugby players, John Eales, Nick Farr-Jones and Andre Agassi. Great leaders, brilliant sportsmen and very successful at business.

In a game of Soccer/Football even the most dominant teams will only have possession, or be in the positive or attacking phase of play for 60% of the time. What that means is that everyone will be dealing with defensive play for a fair portion of the game.

In sport or in life, get ready for what comes next.
In our team the quicker we can turnaround a position the quicker we can react to the changing circumstances in the game.

The elements to great defence are the ability to scramble and react to new situations while remaining organised, the ability to know where your team mates are and how to use them to the best effect. Strong Leadership, supporting your team mates and a willingness to put your self on the line to defend.

Lucas Neill, the former captain of the Socceroos, is one of the great defensive players our country has produced. He is constantly alert, never ever gives up on his job, he is a leader and leads by example, he trains relentlessly and constantly acquires new skills by playing in different leagues. He is organised, disciplined and equal parts nurturing, creates high expectations for his team mates and holds them accountable to achieving them.

When under attack he does not panic but knows what his job is. He organises those around him while he is also doing his own job.

So transition out of defence is already in the mind of the players while they are defending.

Once they have the advantage to move out of a defensive phase of play he acts very quickly. Whether that is by a fast counter attack to take advantage of a disorganised opponent or by maintaining possession of the ball while his offensive players move to an advantageous position. Either way he is thinking about the attacking phase almost before he is finished with the defence.

In fact, when they are right in the most intense part of defending the attack they are prepared for the transition. If they react with a knee jerk response this will likely prolong the defensive phase.

For example: If he just kicked the crap out of the ball and put it back into the opponents half, that would momentarily relive the attack. However the other team would simply control the ball and within seconds you would be defending again.

If however he could gain control of the ball and maintain possession by passing to team mates that are not under pressure from opposition, then the opposition is suddenly chasing the ball. They have moved from attack to defence instantly and if Lucas Neill's team can be more organised, then they can make the opposition run around chasing the ball while his attackers get into positions where they don't have any pressure. Moving into space where you can make a creative decision about how you choose to attack the goal.

Playing above the line

CHAPTER 11.
TRUE COMMUNICATION IS THE RESPONSE I GET: LEARNING TO CONTROL MY BEHAVIOUR

When I'm not getting the responses I want from the team first I need to look at my communication. It' likely to be the starting point of the responses I'm getting back.

If I'm not getting what I want then I keep altering my communication until I get the response I want. The power to change the response I'm getting rests totally with me. And that's the essence of playing above the line. If I need the situation changed, I need to take responsibility and change it.

One evening there was a little unrest in the team. It showed because a few of the players were getting quite upset at each other and it was starting to turn ugly. I see this happening a lot in teams I coach when one of the members has had a bad day and they can bring their frustration to the training field. It happens at work as well.

For example, someone might just ask an innocent question of a colleague and they get their head bitten off. That response doesn't have a lot to do with the question but with whatever went on in both their lives before the question was asked. I call that bringing baggage into the situation. You had a fight with your teenage daughter before you arrived at work and Bam you just tore the head off one of your work mates. They didn't deserve it, they were just in the wrong place at the time and you snapped.

In some teams I have worked with there seems to be a member who likes winding people up.

This kind of team member likes to argue everything, they like to point out any inconsistencies they have picked up on, and they love to get a rise out of others around them. Especially the leader of a group. And it seems to be very important that their every idea, thought and opinion is expressed and a lot of it sounds like criticism.

If they would bring something constructive to the situation you could let it pass, but the constant barrage of counter opinion, often not having much in the way of substance, can be quite undermining to the team and a leader.

It's not just the leader they like to get a rise out of, but also anyone on the team. I have experienced all sorts of people who are various combinations of combative, competitive, intelligent and often extremely capable.. In other words, they contribute to the technical work of the team but can have quite a negative effect on the team culture if allowed to go unchecked.

What this kind of character is especially unskilled at is understanding people and their reactions to the "constructive criticism" they offer. Most of all these kinds of people struggle to control themselves when things aren't going their way.

They seem to be full of bravado and total confidence.

One night at training we had a situation brewing and I went over to find out what was going. A few of the guys were really very angry with Josh. The taunts during practice had been coming thick and fast and it got a little too much for one of the team, so he retaliated, tackling Josh much too hard, then following it up with a little verbal barrage.

Of course Josh claimed innocence and used the situation to direct the blame toward the other player. "I didn't do anything, I don't know what he's getting so upset about"

These type of people like to set the fire, light the fuse and now then stand back and watch it explode.

Only that's not what happened.

I took him aside and started to ask him some questions. Which he didn't like at all.

"So who do you think is in control of the way people respond to you?" I asked him.

"I don't know, I have no control over how someone reacts" he shot back

"So If I spoke to you in a gentle, more friendly way, what do you think your natural response would be?"

"I suppose I'd be friendly back"

"And If I barked orders at you, ignored what you wanted and treated you badly, how would you feel like responding to me then?"

"I'd probably want to tell you to get stuffed" he responded.

"So it would be a fairly aggressive and antagonistic response then?"

"I suppose so"

"In that scenario who was in control of the response?"

"You were"...and at this point he could see where I was going with this and he was getting very antsy, trying to get back to the game

that had continued to go on without him.

"So if you talk to your team mates like they don't matter to you and treat them in a way that tells them you think they are no good how do you think they'll respond to you?"

"Dunno"

"Do you think it would look like what we just saw?"

Silence…

"So who is responsible for the reaction. Him or you?"

More silence

"If you are willing to change the way you talk to him you can rejoin the game. Otherwise take a break until you are prepared to do that"

"I think I'll take a break coach" and he went off to cool down.

One thing I always appreciated about Josh was that when he knew he was wrong and I confronted him about it, he copped it on the chin.

He wasn't happy about it and certainly didn't want to talk about it, but he'd usually say "fair enough" and then start playing above the line again. This is one of the reasons I had a soft spot for him.

That's exactly what happened here. He cooled down and started playing again 5 mins later without winding his team mates up.

Apparently he'd had a tough day. I'm not sure why and he never explained, but he was taking it out on one of his team mates and that's just not o.k. He was carrying some leftover emotion from somewhere else and was unloading it on his teammates, where it just wasn't called for. He was directing his frustration and anger in the wrong place. I see this happen in work groups, families and bands all the time.

The communication he got back was a reflection of the way he was communicating to others.

When we are in blame mode we often get really hostile communications back from others. This is the true reflection of the communication you are giving out. The power is entirely with you to change that. If you want a different response, start communicating in the way you want to see it returned.

This is a classic example of accepting responsibility for the relationships around you and taking ownership of the method of communicating with each other.

Learning To Listen

People think listening is just the absence of talking, but nothing could be further from the truth.

It's an active process, and the true art of listening is about understanding what the other has said, reflecting back to them that you've understood, then digging deeper to understand at a deeper level what you are listening to.

Listening is not waiting for a gap in the conversation for you to talk about yourself or give your opinion.

I like to say that listening is like peeling back the layers of an onion. You start the conversation at the surface level, and once someone feels heard and understood they allow you to peel back the other layers and reveal the truths hidden beneath the surface.

People often refer to listening as active listening or reflective listening. That's because it's not passive and requires effort and commitment to be a good listener.

It requires you to put your own agenda and ideology to one side and reflect back to the other person what you've understood the to say, and if you are feeling bold or insightful you might ask a question that reveals what that means as you dig deeper and deeper into the conversation.

People rarely manage to communicate exactly what they think

about a topic in the first instance and it requires you to reflect back to them what you've understood them to say and check in to make certain you've understood it correctly.

If you've ever played Chinese Whispers as a child you will know what I mean.

If you haven't played that game, it goes like this: Everyone starts by sitting in a circle. The object of the game is to get the original message from the first person to the last as accurately as you can. The first whispers the message in the ear of the person next to them, and it's their job to understand what they said and pass it on. Of course, an original message that started as "the small monkey sat on the fence smiling" tends to end up something like "all the money in the bank is mine".

Level of accuracy, Zero.

And this is so often how we communicate in our teams. The message goes from person 1 to person 15 and the meaning has altered irrevocably.

And we have introduced frustration, confusion and a serious lack of clarity in the process.

But if you were to change the rule of one way communication just a tiny bit by allowing the person to check that they've understood what they heard by repeating it back, then the factor of accuracy goes up immeasurably.

That's why in critical situations there is a policy of confirming the command. Particularly in military situations. You see it with astronauts who don't just say copy, but will repeat the entire instruction. Because if you are on a space craft and you misunderstand the instructions just a little, the results are catastrophic.

I feel particularly passionate about listening because learning to listen saved my marriage.

After my wife and I had been married for about 4 or 5 years things started to really go off the rails.

Like so many couples we had expectations of each other that we weren't communicating or even verbalising. We were mad at each other for what looked like an endless litany of trivial things.

But what I discovered underneath it all was that I didn't feel heard, or understood. The result of that was frustration, anger and feeling alienated.

And as it turns out, my wife was feeling the same thing. We were talking to each other but not really listening.

What that meant was if one of us started talking about a subject, we agreed that the other would put aside their feelings about what was being said (no small task) and just reflectively listen, dig deeper, understand what was really going on and give the other the gift of being heard all the way through to the core of the issue.

What I've written in the paragraph above took a fair bit of work to achieve and I think I've made it sound simpler than it was. As with any new skill, we practiced it and got better and better at it. The more we did it the easier it became. The more wins we had with it the more we'd commit to using it.

Right now you are probably thinking, that's all well and good for the person being listened to but what about the other. When do they get to have their turn?

My experience is that there is an undercurrent of reciprocity in relationships and the law we discussed earlier about true communication being the response you get comes into play.

If I put aside my perspectives and ideology about the topic at hand and concentrate on understanding your true feelings on the subject, that will result in you feeling heard, understood and acceptable. And the level of trust in that relationship will have been deepened quite a bit.

You will likely feel that you want to reciprocate and start listening at a deeper level.

The end result of this is that the communication you get back is a direct result of the communication you give out.

You are in total control of the response you get from others.

This is what happened in my marriage. By listening and understanding myself, I received back the same level of understanding and all the endless trivial things that were bothering us melted away because the true cause of frustration was revealed. Everything else was just a symptom.

How This Helped Our Team

When we are playing above the line, we recognise that if we listen to our team mates and understand what is really going on for them, we will create trust at a significantly deeper level.

And best of all you aren't relying on someone else to start this thing off. You can start it.

I'll tell you a little more about how we use that in workgroups in the next book, but for now I had introduced the idea that each member of our team was in total control of the reaction they got from others. This would be very important in some of the very tight matches that would come up in the next few weeks.

Where this idea of communication being the response I get really started to work for us in the coming weeks was in dealing with other teams. If for example; we play rough against another team and tackle late and hurt them, we cannot be surprised that they will retaliate in kind. If we first keep that kind of play out of the game, then we are to the greatest extent possible, controlling the response we get from the opposition.

Is that 2 Bucks?

Staying above the line is a real challenge for our team of Property Managers. They are very, very busy and the pressure of dealing with hundreds of clients who all require your attention can be very demanding and draining. Occasionally we have a little crisis with a clients property or tenant, and then the drama starts. And once the dram starts it seems to escalate. It's infectious and everyone in the office feels it, and often the clients escalate their demands as well.

We have made a "rules of the game" for our office which outlines the way we will behave with each other and it has the promise to play above the line in it. Which means no excuses, no blame and no drama..... We also promised each other that we'd keep each other accountable to that.

When drama and a crisis enters the office that quite difficult to do. Just telling someone that their behaviours is below the line is likely to not end well. So we started a game called Is that Two Bucks?

Everyone agreed that if they slipped below the line the way we would keep each other accountable is to place a small fine for below the line behaviours. So if we caught one of the team mates blaming, making excuses or getting too emotional about a situation we would simply ask.... Is that $2?

What that usually results in is a laugh, and the person saying, yeah it probably is. And then we start focusing on how we can help each other find a solution.

We have a little jar that collects the money and it's in the middle of the office. Even before Brett finished the explanation the boss was caught out and had to chip in $2, which he did with a big laugh.. He even offered to put in $20 to cover him for the day.

It's just a great reminder to everyone that we have all agreed to play our game at another level.

Authors note:
Marshal Thurber was the originator of this game, and I believe the creator of the Above the Line model, and he used the game to

Playing above the line

create huge change in large organisations.

There is a really cool YouTube video of him describing what he did. If you search under the term "is that 2 bucks" you'll find it.

He did it in a very large organisation and the game was intended as a way to keep everyone above the line. They decided that any money they were fined would go to a charity. I understand they donated about $250,000 to the charity of their choice, and transformed the culture of the organisation.

Staying above the line requires daily discipline. It's not enough to just know about it, you must put it into action every day. And this requires us to keep each other accountable. Knowledge without action is not worth a dot. I think the Dali Lama said it much more poetically than that.

When I first suggested the idea of this game the immediate reaction from the team was near horror. I don't want to have to pay $2 every time I slip up......

But that's just the point, small amounts of money can create large change.

I was recently doing some work with Marshall Goldsmith, who is a worldwide authority on behavioural change. He works with very senior executives and he told me this story.

"When I start working with CEO's I make a game with some rules, and if they break the rules I fine them $20. They really, really don't like it. They whine and carry on about having to put in $20 when they infringe the rules. Now these guys are earning $10-50 Million a year, they can afford it. But it doesn't stop them complaining and resenting the fines. The money will even go to a charity of their choice. One of my clients was even photographed recently handing over a cheque to his charity for $200,000.

So what's this reaction about?

The truth is no one likes loosing, not even a small amount of money. And that's my opportunity to help them change behaviour quickly. On day one this game might cost them $200, because they keep displaying the behaviour we agreed would trigger the fine. Then day 2 it only costs them $60, Day 3, $20 and pretty soon it doesn't cost them anything at all. Small amounts of money can cause large change."

And this is why the $2 game is so effective. And if $2 is too much make it something smaller. $1 or 20 cents.

Make a fun game out of to and you will find this a great way to maintain change and stay above the line.

Playing above the line

CHAPTER 12.
THE RETURN OF COACH X

We completed the season as clear premiers. Now it was time for the play-offs. In Soccer you get 3 points for a win, 1 for a draw and 0 for a loss.

We were in front of the nearest team by 15 points. In other words, we could have lost 4 more games and still won. It's a lead that is extraordinary for a team that by all assessments is no better man for man than our nearest 3 or 4 teams.

In Australian sports, we have the normal round of approximately 14 games with the winner being called the premiers or in some codes Minor Premiers. Then we have the finals round. The top 4 teams play off against each other for the Grand Final and the winner of that is called the champion team. Not every country does it this way but it makes the last few rounds a playoff of the best of the best in each division. If the math's is with you and the result of the other games works in your favour, then you can still scrape through to the Grand Final. And that's a big deal.

Playing above the line

The night before the Grand Final I was hardly able to sit still, let alone sleep soundly. A million scenarios were going through my head and I was creating a plan for everyone of them. Who would start, who would sub and when to rotate the subs. How would we deal with their attacks and would my team hold it together under the pressure of Grand Final day.

But the biggest question for me was could they hold it all together and keep the biggest weapon we had going. Could they continue to play above the line under the most intense pressure they had faced yet.

For these young people the pressure was enormous; the desire to outdo their initial goal and cap off a brilliant season.

But they were playing against the team that had come 2nd and they were quite good. They deserved to hold that position. Last year the guys who stood opposite us now had blitzed the entire division winning both the premiership and the championship, they were good and they were accustomed to winning. This was the team that one of my mates coaches. This is the team that he correctly assessed that they were almost an equal match for us skill for skill, and their least skilled players were certainly better than our least skilled players. He had mentioned to me earlier in the season that the only thing that separated us was our ability to communicate and work together as a team. The unwavering support that we had for each other and the determination to be totally responsible for what each player contributed. There was no blame and no justification in our players. Just quick corrections, rather than failures. This is what he observed was the difference between our teams..... But could they hold it together for the final test? This was what was keeping me awake and this is the first thought that went through my head as I woke much earlier than I wanted to on the Grand Final morning. What would I need to do to keep them playing above the line for this final challenge?

The Grand Final day is quite an event. It's everything you picture in your mind and probably what movies draw their inspiration from. The grounds are buzzing, streamers, banners, supporters everywhere and every game on every field is played for high stakes. The opportunity to lift the trophy or go home empty handed. Supporters, families and friends come from everywhere to cheer on their team. Often big banners are made, flags are waving and the atmosphere is electric. In the mind of a child this is a big, big deal. And something you really want to experience if you play sport.

At the end of each game is a presentation ceremony where speeches are made, commiserations are spoken and trophies and medals are distributed. It's quite something. And this was our goal, our mission. To be part of that day. Not necessarily to win it, just to be part of it. To give that experience to these wonderful teenagers is something I wanted for them very much. And what stood in our way was 2 more games, and the first game we drew was against Mr. X and his team.

I knew this could be a bit ugly. The way their team behaved had not improved throughout the season. They had the highest record for infringements and yellow and red cards in the entire age group. Their tactics had worked because they were now in the playoffs for a berth in the Grand Final. But the way they play and conduct themselves is so totally opposite to everything I had learned about what makes a winning team, that I found myself really wanting to make a point.

One big difference in a team like this is that they will mercilessly exclude any player in their team that wont get them a result. So many of the less skilled players in the team will find themselves sitting on the bench throughout the last few games, watching the action and wondering why they aren't being included. And I cannot think of a more soul destroying way to be treated as a young guy or girl.

What this would also mean is that the most gnarly, aggressive and egregious players in coach X's team would be starting the game today. Their giant players, at least 4 of them 6 foot 2 inches tall, would be facing up against my guys and girls, most of whom had not yet had their teenage growth spurt yet. While their average team height was closer to 6 feet tall, ours was much closer to 5 foot 6. When they lined up for the refs instructions at the beginning of the game we looked a little like David coming up against Goliath.

Playing above the line

To make things more challenging, we were playing on their home field which was way over the other end of town and 3 of our team had not yet found the field. And the game was about to begin. We were playing one player short against these giants.

So the preparation warm-up was a little challenging with everyone focusing on whether we were going to be able to field a full team or not. We looked a bit like a rabble and that's not the unified team I wanted to present to the opposition.

Just before kick off and after they had warmed up, I took them away from the crowd to a quiet part of the field and had a quick chat.

In the quiet of the field, with our supporter on one side of us and the opposition and officials on the other, I told them how proud I was of them and what a legendary team of players they were. Not just for the results they had achieved but for the way they had done it. For the teamwork that they had showed week after week.

I believed with all my heart that today they could win this Grand Final as long as they did three things;

"Stay above the line. And don't allow blame or excuses into your game. Support your team mates with every once of energy you have, then come and rest. Let someone else go on and take over for a little while. Recover and go and do it all over again.

You guys are leaders, every last one of you, and there are a lot of people here to see you in action.

So show them what got you here, show them what a team looks like when it's in full flight, show them what you are capable of not only as soccer players, but as amazing young men and women… and know that we are immensely proud of you."

The whistle blew and they were off to their big adventure.

Just as the game started, Suzie arrived who brought our height average down as she is about 5 foot 1 inch but has a heart that is twice as big as anyone on our team. I threw her straight on without any warm-up. At least we could match them in numbers.

The first few minutes of the game are tense as each team search out the strengths and weaknesses of the opposition. One of my weaknesses was that I had 2 players lost in the suburbs texting me about where the field was and my focus was certainly split between the game and the missing players.
Coach X just stood about 4 meters away with 5 subs next to him, each one hoping for his anointment to go and have a run on the field. I stood there with no subs and a team who were demonstrating a very high work rate to outplay these guys, so they were going to wear out fast.

What's more, I refused to exclude the lesser skilled players and made sure they had as good a run as they were capable of, so I had some of my best players on the field and some of my weakest, everyone of them giving 100% to the team and putting themselves on the line to contribute.

Despite her size, Suzie rarely allowed a player to get past her. You could see the slightly cocky look in the opposition players eye as he approached Suzie, probably thinking, oh this will be easy. But before they knew what had happened, Suzie had picked their pocket and they were running without the ball. Or they would come in hard thinking she would flinch…she didn't and they were quite surprised to see how resilient she was. The one disadvantage she did have was that it's hard to keep pace with a giant with long legs, but that's where her team had her back. If her opposite number was getting away from her she would very quickly have one of the faster guys covering her and with fierce loyalty they would stand behind her in support.

I never once heard any negative word from any of the guys about having a girl on the team. I think, actually one or two of the boys thought she was pretty cute. I only ever heard "Well done Suzie", saw the guys high fiving her after a great tackle and encouraging her. And that's what our team played like. No smashing each other, no anger or frustration, no blame and no excuses. Just a lot of well done's.

Playing above the line

Well Done

And this was on purpose.
In a book that I have been hugely influenced by called "Whale Done", which is co-authored by Ken Blanchard, he describes a totally new way to get your team motivated and working together. And it turns out that it builds on one of the leadership principals. Give attention to the behaviour that you want to see more of. Teach the team the power of positive praise and you will see a significant change in behaviour that is more helpful to creating a winning team.

What the Authors of the book "Whale Done" suggest is that "The more attention you pay to a behaviour, the more it will be repeated" and, "If you don't want to encourage poor behaviour, don't spend a lot of time on it.".

The key is to focus on what reaction or consequence you are giving rather the outcome. If you give positive reaction to a behaviour that you want to see more of then it will happen again and again. If you get a behaviour that is undesirable, don't give it any attention.

This helps build trust by accentuating the positive, and when mistakes or undesirable behaviour occur you redirect the energy.

Redirection

Redirection works like this: You identify the challenge or behaviour without blame. Clearly identify the negative impact of this and outline the better way to handle it. Then praise the first step toward the new goal; always praising incrementally, not waiting until they fully achieved the new outcome.

In Soccer, one of the things that really takes away from the team experience and the success of the game is when one player hogs the ball and will not pass it. I've seen it so many times over the years and it is contrary to the spirit of the game and absolutely destroys a teams ability to win. It's not the same as taking risks and seizing opportunities.

Classically when one player hogs the ball, or holds it too long they are in their own little world, trying to beat this player and then the next, all the time drawing attention to how wonderful they are. I have come to see this as an attention seeking tactic. I guess they are hoping they will finally beat all the opposition to put the ball into the net and be hoisted onto the shoulders of their team mates and hailed as a hero…that's the fantasy in their heads anyway.

In reality, no matter how good you are, the opposition will eventually work out how to stop you. Using an entire team to stop one player who they know won't pass the ball is one of the easiest things to defend against.

What is far more difficult to defend against is a team who hold the ball for one or two touches, or a fraction of a second, and then off-load it to their team mates who have moved into space while their opposite numbers are chasing the ball.

But that's a very difficult thing to convince a child to do. Creating a culture where each member of the team is acknowledged for their contribution is not often accomplished, so in comes the "Whale Done" approach.

Praise the attention you want to see more of and give no attention to the behaviour you want to discourage. So when a player hogs the ball and takes 8 or 10 touches before loosing the ball to the opposition, they get no attention. When they pass the ball off quickly they get lots of praise.

In some families they will reward their son or daughter with money every time they score a goal. So this makes it very, very challenging to encourage the team behaviour. In one team I coached, our striker was given $5 for every goal he scored. So when he was even within sight of the goal he would never, ever pass off that ball. He was giving away an opportunity for $5 after all. He would hold the ball while all of his team mates were standing near him with no defenders between them and the goal, but do you think he would pass the ball or go for the impossible attempt on goal? It became so frustrating for one father who was standing on the side line that he couldn't help himself. *"Oh! for *%$#'s sake will you give him $10 if he passes the ball in front of*

Playing above the line

goal?".
Praise the assist. That's one of the critical elements in creating a winning team. That way you will encourage the behaviours that will win the match. The goal scorers could not put the ball in the back of the net without the help of everyone on the team.

The Game In Front Of Us

Coach X was doing his usual trick, surly, hunched over, arms crossed, loud and negative. Barking every time his team committed a misdemeanour. Giving attention to every mistake, every foul, late tackle, push in the back and illegal behaviour. So guess what he got more of. All that crap.

My plan was to give attention to all the behaviour that was opposite and far more constructive to winning this game. Every fast pass, every backup move that one of our guys did, every tackle that allowed our team to catch up, when they did a recovery run back to position despite how tired they were, every time they moved into space and every time an attacking player looked like they were about to shoot for goal and at the last moment, offloaded it to their team mate waiting at the back post to put that ball into the net. If the play started from the goalie through the backs, mid's and then forwards I praised every single one of them equally, not just the goal scorer. It was to me the ultimate expression of "we win as a team and we lose as a team".

It was a tough game and despite the fact we had no substitutes for the first 10 minutes we were ahead 1:0. Coach X was livid. His pasty complexion was turning pink, the veins on his neck were pulsing and I could see we were going to have to work hard but the thing we had that they didn't was a willingness to work together as a team.

They would use their best player, who was formidable, as an attacking cruise missile. Putting the ball out in front for him to pick up, out muscle our guys and potentially get a shot at a goal. But he was just one guy. They didn't have anyone to help him or back him up. When he would take a run Coach X would be screaming for the rest of his team to back him up, but they knew he wasn't going to pass the ball to them so they eventually ran out of steam and put up with the abuse from their coach. They were relying on a champion player to win them the game, but they were coming up against a champion team.

Yes their start player was big, fast and talented. But when we worked out how they were playing, I saw my backs developing strategies to deal with him. First they double teamed him. One player to hold him up and another player to be a 2nd defender in case he slipped the first. They also defended in such a way that he ended up way out on the sideline with nearly our whole defensive line between him and the goal and almost no help from his team. It became a dead end for him. Our brilliant right back, Sam, would wear him down, knowing he had his team at his back if he needed them, eventually get the ball away from him and then counter attack very quickly. It was a joy to see the way they organised themselves to deal with this threat.

This game was taking it's toll on my guys and they were getting tired. It was a physical and exhausting game. Finally, our extra 2 players arrived. They had found the field. Hallelujah! But as they arrived we had let our guard down for a moment and they managed to slip one past us to make it 1:1.

I made our late arrivals warm up for 10 minutes before allowing them onto the field, not just because I didn't want them injured, but I wanted them to observe the game while they were warming up. It's as much a game of psychology as it is a physical game and I wanted them tuned in to what their team mates were doing.

They finally ran on, replacing my 2 most tired defenders with only about 15 minute to go in the half. We had some fresh legs, an opportunity to cycle the team around and refresh.

The tactics the opposition seemed to be employing was to go harder, louder and more aggressively. I suspect that this was their one and only tactic they had learned from coach X. But it had drawn them level with us, so they just kept on pushing.

The half time whistle blew, we were level and a little nervous...
The half time ritual began; What are we doing best? And what do

Playing above the line

we need to be doing better?

We decided that the best way to deal with these guys was to limit our passes to a maximum of three touches each. Two touches if possible. What that means is a fast game. You get very little time to control the ball before you need to visualise the next move, then execute it before you get hammered by the opposition giants.

It requires commitment from everyone because your team mates need to give you options for your next pass to your left, right, near in front of you and far in front. And you need to change each of those positions about every 2 seconds. Even once you've made the pass you need to be ready to receive it back. There is no rest, it's technically challenging to maintain that level of concentration and physical exertion for a full 40 minutes. They decided to go for it. I double checked, *"Are you sure you are willing to go this road?"* *"Yes Coach"* they replied. *"That means if you are tired you must come off for a break, are you willing to do that?"* *"Absolutely coach".*

My team had decided this tactic for themselves, it hadn't been pushed on them. So that meant they were fully committed to the approach. This proved to be a huge difference in the teams. My team had agreed on a strategy and set about executing it well. It came from them and all I did was help them to understand the parameters of what that meant. The opposition team had a vision for the game pushed on them by a coach who took a dictatorial approach. We could see many of the team didn't agree with it and were not committed to the approach their coach had made them take. This was to prove to be one of the critical differences, when the strategy and vision for the job in front of us comes from within the team they are vastly more committed to the mission.

Here is the match report from our resident wit and somewhat subjective chronographer of our games.

Saturday 7th June

Saints 3-1 v's The Giants

Again, another great win. We knew that this was going to be another tough game. Early on we were passing and holding possession well. We were even creating opportunities. In the early minutes of the game, William somehow skied one (shot the ball over the goal) from right in front of the goal, just as he did the last time we versed this team. It's like he doesn't want to score against these guys. But that gave us a morale boost and the confidence to keep the pressure on.

I think that our pressure was a key point to the win. We shut them down almost instantaneously and gave them no opportunity to run freely. Something that they could not do to us. Andy would like to say he got a hat trick, however, he really got two goals and an assist, as the first goal was in fact an own goal which was set up by Cody and helped on its way by Andy. Throughout the first half, there were many chances on our part created by Andy, Hayden, William, Vincent and Cody. Something that we did well was taking shots, with Hayden, Josh, Vincent and William all having a go. We also did well in locking the ball into their half. This allowed us to keep a high line of defence and keep the attack going. Sam, Tyler, Ryan and Johnno did well in helping the attack and the defence when necessary. Eddie and Tyler did very well in holding the defence and controlling the middle of the park. Easts did bring it back to 1-1 which had us nervous. It was very evenly balanced with attacks from both teams but no more goals before the break. Jack made a courageous save, diving on the ball with what seemed to be 12 opposition players around him.

No more goals until the deadly duo of Hayden and Vincent. Hayden put another great cross in for Vincent who tucked it away with a brilliant header, which seemed to have some sort of effect on their keeper. After his little dummy-spit, Cody thought he would have a go, made a great run and crossed the ball low and hard into Andy who was standing unopposed at the back post and he put the ball in the back of their net. By this time we knew that we could hold on for the win which was a great relief. There were nutties and some flair from all our players as the game was all but over. Even Suzie had a shot.

Special mention to Thomos for his header and for his ever amusing hairstyles.

The end of this game was one of the most personally satisfying for me. It was mentally, emotionally and physically tough for my team and for me. We had used both technical skills and team skills to overcome the giant of Coach X's team, and we had finished it 3:1.

We were very likely on our way to the Grand Final. One of the most rambunctious and opinionated boys came over to me and in an uncharacteristically candid moment said *"thanks Brett, you are a really good coach"*.

This is a boy who had fought me all the way on tactics, training, always had an opinion about how we should play and who should play where on the field, and is continuing to push me as we enter the next season. This is a boy who has a hot temper and loves to get attention by winding people up. But right now, he was enjoying the moment that we overcame another huge obstacle and played like a champion team.

I was speechless at first, it was totally unexpected, I resisted the urge to take the micky out of him, and Instead put my arm around his shoulders and said "you were magnificent today, well done mate".

His was a transformation from a boy who believed that to win they needed to be individual champions. He was finishing the season understanding what it meant to play in a champion team.

Here is my match report of the game which is often published to balance the somewhat subjective versions from our man on the ground.

Hey Team
You all had a brilliant game on Saturday. I suspected it was going to be tough. And they proved us right.

They defended well and their goalie was quite skilful (although had nothing on Jack).

Everyone battled well and showed a never give up spirit.

The second half was particularly intense. Especially when we got in front, and their attack lifted. But our defence lifted even more to hold them out.

The entire team gave 110% in the second half.

The backs had a fantastic game. Sam had a huge battle with a guy at least 15cm taller than him, and he won it every time.

Suzie was unbelievable and brave as she was bumped around quite a bit by her opposite number and never blinked for a moment. And really forced them to play around her every time.

Tyler was formidable in the centre, I think they are running around you on purpose because they don't want to face your wrath. Johnno your calm control of the ball is wonderful and we love to see you take on the defenders, round them with poise and hoof the ball upfield. Actually, you played some really good short passes under pressure and completed them every time.

Eddie; words don't quite describe your effort. You and Jack had the back line working like a well oiled machine and you were leading by example, never stopping once to take on every challenge. After the game Eddie looked totally spent and I think you used every last ounce you had keeping the score line with us in front.

Jack. I'm so pleased we had you in goals in the 2nd half, we needed your skill and calm. I saw you pluck the ball out of harms way at least 3 times. The entire sideline breathed a huge sigh of relief when you did.

Our defending mids worked very hard, with Daniel and Diago giving it all they had. In the end both of them were exhausted but cheered the final minutes from the sideline. Supporting the team even from the sideline.

Hayden, I've got to disagree with Johnno, you are the energizer bunny of the team. Never giving up or giving in. Despite a sniper taking your feet out from under you, And your corners are sublime. Without your poised and perfectly weighted crosses we wouldn't have got up.

Vincent... Love the use of your head in the goal area. (I'm resisting a Johnno like comment about using your head for something useful) I think they weren't going to allow a goal along the ground but you chose a great spot in what was probably their only weakness. We were not taller than them but when you rose in the middle of the pack you showed more heart than the opposition. You and Hayden are a lethal combination.

Josh, what a brilliant run you had on the left. We had the joy of watching the battle close up, and it was brilliant. Even when they put 2 men on you they couldn't contain you. Your speed and tenacity were brilliant. And your support for all the team mates around you was unwavering.

William your strength in controlling the midfield was strong under constant attack. They never let up on you and you never stopped. Brilliant.

Thomas, The Hair had everyone talking, and probably the opposition guessing as well. Was it a brilliant ruse to keep the opposition talking about your hair while you stole the ball away and played around them to join in yet another attack... Hmmm, certainly a discussion point. Do we have any volunteers for the same tactic?

Andy, as ever, awesome captain work, despite the incorrect shorts (must lead by example) and the speed which you ran across to put pressure on the goalie was awesome. How you had that much fuel in the tank I just don't know. Your pace and control down the line draws out the opposition giving the remainder of the team some precious space in the middle. And your full frontal attack in the first few minutes of the game put everyone on notice that it was game on.

The thing which is working so well is your team work. You are fast *becoming a champion team. When you work so well together, always giving 100% and never leaving your team mates without supported, we don't need a $35M marquee import.*

A champion team will win every time over a team of individual champions every time.

I'm very proud of you all.
Regards Brett

P.S. Cody and Ryan, we hope to see you back next week. You were missed.

Playing above the line

CHAPTER 13.
LESSONS WE LEARNED: OUR GRAND FINAL

"The world is not yet a crazy enough place to reward a bunch of undeserving people. To get what you want you must deserve what you want" Charlie Munger

"So show them what got you here, show them what a team looks like when it's in full flight, show them what you are capable of, not only as soccer players, but as amazing young men and women...and know that we are immensely proud of you." Brett's speech to the team as they went on to the field for the Grand Final.

Email from Brett to the team prior to the Grand Final, August 2014.
They had just earned the right to play in the Grand Final.

What a spectacular game you all played yesterday and it was a brilliant way to end the season. Having achieved our goal we set out to do..... To get to the Grand Final.

Playing above the line

And having achieved some amazing additional goals. To win the premiership undefeated and to have won the Jim Collins Shield for the highest performing team in the club this year. Out of about 50 teams and nearly 800 players that's quite something.

More importantly than all of that, you have become a champion team; A team that always supports one another on and off the field and always gives 100%. Keeping each other above the line and taking responsibility for your contribution and having a fantastic time while doing it.

We set and maintained a culture of respect for each other, the refs decisions (although sometimes questionable) and the opposition. You played the game beautifully and as the opposition coach said to me yesterday...you all deserve to be at the Grand Final.
I am so proud of each and everyone of you. It has been an absolute honour to be your coach this year.

You are a legendary team, with heart and spirit that is the envy of many in the club and opposite you on the field. Each one of you are leaders and have shown time and time again what the very best of teams look like.

Thank you all for an amazing season.

Next week is our Grand Final and I am very much looking forward to your performance and to see more of what you have shown us all year. Exactly what a champion team looks like.

You will have a lot of people from the club coming down to watch the game. Many of the adults I play with have followed you throughout the year and are coming to watch you next week. Soak up the atmosphere and enjoy.

See you all at training. Brett

The Grand Final match report by one of our team members, and resident dry wit.

It was introduced by the team manager like this.

Hi team,

Congratulations on a fantastic win yesterday - it capped off a wonderful season. The final match report is attached and I want to thank Johno for writing them all (in his unique objective style).

Saints 5-1 Norths

A glorious end to the year. The best in the comp.

Well done.

From the outset, it seemed like it was going to be a tough game with an early shot from the oppositions star striker and all round good guy Tim. However, it was not to be. Within the two minutes Vincent scored off a lovely run from Andy which was set up, originally, by Eddie. Right from our center back through our midfield up to our striker. It was a fantastic start. The attitude did not change with another attack coming from the Saints. This time through Cody with a great goal after some nice team play. It was all fun and games with William, technically a defender at the time with a miracle volley of which even the greats (Ronaldo, Ibra, Messi, Pele) would have been proud.

After this quick flurry of goals from our team, Norths caught on and defended well. They had some attacking opportunities and even some shots. Some of the defending efforts weren't so good from the Saints and some shots got quite close. Jack had to make some miraculous saves and they weren't easy, in fact, they were fantastic saves. He just couldn't keep his hands off those balls?

Even with all our excellent defending and goalkeeping power, we were not able to keep Norths from scoring. (actually the author of the match report was mucking around and showing off a little with a play that was a little too tricky, he lost the ball and we were punished). Some doubt of, "could we hold on?" crept into our minds. These thoughts vanished though, right after kick off when we held the ball nicely and passed it around well. This led to a somewhat fortunate goal after Cody shot straight into the keeper, luckily for Cody, the keeper fumbled and it rolled into the bottom corner.

A ball comes out to Johnno (he's the author and a little prone to egocentricity) after a Norths attack. He controls it and runs it part way down the left wing. A quick one two with H-Bomb leaves Norths dumbfounded, some sweet tekkers to beat 3 opposition players from Johnno allows him to set up a pass to Hayden who shoots and misses but Andy is there to clean up the mess after some confusion in the box to make it 5-1. At this point, we started to relax. We were playing games with their number 8 (midfielder) and having great time watching them get mad. It ended up being a fairly one sided game but could have been much closer if it wasn't for Jack, (our goalie). He made some fantastic saves during the game and really separated us from Norths.

MOTM - Jack for an outstanding performance in goal and "The game of his life" as the opposing coach said.

Special mention - William for a close second for MOTM and a brilliant game in the middle.

(what a surprise that a teenager would nominate himself for second MOTM, see what I've got to work with ☺)

Moment of the Season - Well, it had to be Diago's goal against Glenhaven for the fact that it kept us undefeated and the shock factor of having Diago scoring the most important goal of the season.

Player of the season - Andy for making about 1000 runs down the right side and creating and scoring lots of goals.

I take cash or credit and if anyone wants this done next season its $50 each, thank you and goodbye - Johnno

Finally
In his own way he just about summed up the season. You can hear the pride, fun and sense of mastery he feels. And this is a boy that has played for less than 12 months when we started the season.

They won the Grand Final 5:1, a huge victory!

As they have all season, they played like a champion team and the opposition just didn't have an answer for it. The captain of my team made an interesting comment at half time. He said the opposition team and their supporters on the opposite sideline were so far below the line that they were below the line that's below the line. Actually, he postulated, they were of the page.

Triple Winners

This team won the premiership, the championship and were undefeated. We had certainly achieved far greater than I had expected and way, way beyond what we had done any previous year.

All this achieved with a bunch of players that are no more technically skilled than any of their opposition, and in some cases much less skilled. More and more I'm inspired by what a team can achieve

They also won the Club Shield, which is a club trophy for the top performing team out of nearly 800 players and about 50 Teams. It is a perpetual trophy that lives in the clubhouse as it has done for nearly 70 years now. It now has the names of all 17 players of this winning team inscribed on it forever. And as others in our club have done, they may one day point it out to their children and tell stories of what it felt like to play in a winning team.

A champion team.

I asked some of the guys what they learnt this year and what was most valuable to them. This was their reply.

Everyone one of them said a version of the following

- Communication is key.
- Play above the line. Be responsible for what you do.
- Be supportive of your team mates.
- No blame and no excuses.
- Sometimes you need to go back before going forward.
- Talking and Cooperation can lift the spirit of the team and make you a better player.

- And never, ever, ever give up!

CHAPTER 14.
THE 7 LESSONS

These are the 7 things that made a difference to our team.

1. We had a **common goal** and a **clarity of purpose** that everyone agreed on.

2. **A culture that supports the team & the individual members** and means everyone comes together. We made **agreements with each other**, about our behaviour, and we held each other accountable to those agreements. So that we only had to manage the agreements not the players. It set up an environment within the team that brought out the best in each of us.

3. **Leadership requires selflessness, courage and tenacity.** A definition I have of a leader is that people flourish and grow around them. Leaders help their team to never, never, never give up. So members feel totally

supported.

4. **We took responsibility for our own contribution**..... No blame, no excuses and no drama. This empowered everyone in our team, and we held each other accountable for our actions.

5. **No mistakes, only feedback. No failure only feedback**: So we corrected fast and we fixed things without any recrimination. This meant players could take risks and act on inspiration without fear of being torn down. We did not blame, attack or put down anyone for taking a risk that didn't work out.

6. **What gets attention will be repeated.** We rewarded the behaviour we wanted to see more of. We did not come down on bad behaviour we just did not acknowledge behaviour we wanted to see less of. This corrected the behaviour without punishing people. This built a huge amount of trust between the team and coach. We praised progress, risk, inspiration, teamwork, tenacity and assistance everywhere we saw it.

7. **True communication is the response I get:** As a team we were aware of and took responsibility for the quality of our communication.

This book is a story of how a group of young men and women **started from behind the eight ball and became a winning team.**

They achieved a level of performance that even shocked themselves...

...And it's a parable for our lives and our work.

This group took total responsibility for their individual contribution...

......and eliminated blame, excuses and drama from their work.

In other words.....They learned to play above the line

And they had the turnaround performance of their lives.

I work with groups because working in a team can be a transformational experience.

Working in a group that is Connected, Committed, and Courageous, in an environment where you feel invincible, where your team has your back and will never, never, never give up on you.

Well..... It's pretty cool.

This is where you can be the best version of yourself.

And I wonder if it might not be the antidote to the loneliness, frustration and the self absorbed destructiveness that is plaguing our modern culture and our workplaces.

And I feel it's especially important for our young men and women

I have a passion to introduce this system to more groups.

And if you want to help me, pass this book on, or just teach someone you know what playing above the line means.

It doesn't matter too much if you don't get it perfect; just know for now that **you are powerful beyond measure when you choose to take responsibility for yourself, your actions, your communications, your happiness.**

And progress is better than perfection

Why teams?

Because everyone experiences a team almost every day

It's not just the professional athletes you see on television being paid lots of money that work in teams. Most people experience a team at work, school or on a local sporting field on the weekend.

It could be at church, your community, a drama group, film set or a musical group… even a rock and roll band is one of the tightest teams you will ever see.

Your family is probably your most important team in your life.

Team is all around us every day; it's in our DNA. We are social animals and we are wired to connect with others in our tribe.

But very few people have experienced working together in a team that is so effortless, so smooth, so harmonious that you seem to read each others mind?

When this happens, this is called synergy…..and it's magic.

When this happens it fills me with joy and deep satisfaction because I have connected with my mates and contributed to something greater than me. And in return I have received… what I'd best call grace.

Unfortunately many people don't experience teams this way.

Most people I've spoken to tell me that they've never experienced a team like that.

What they have experienced is a soul crushing, rule orientated, fear inducing group environment where they are afraid to make mistakes for fear of being ridiculed and embarrassed by an overworked, over bearing, hyper critical…… you know what.

People never take a chance in an environment like that.
They won't take responsibility and they lose all motivation to turn up…. Which is kind of ok if you are part of a social group or a casual sporting team.

But it's NOT OK if you have to turn up to work like that each day, or worse you go home to that each night.

In the new world ….. you are either growing or dying. Your team is either coming together or you are, ever so slowly, falling apart.

And unless you keep working to bring your team together and continue to stand up for what you believe; hold very tight to your values, your team is in danger of loosing it's synergy, and it's focus and will begin to fall apart.

And here's the thing…. the hard fact: If you come up against a team that has synergy, a team that takes responsibility for their work and play above the line. You will lose.

You will look at them and wonder why it seems so easy. After all you'll have very talented people on your team, experienced, skilled and driven people and still you won't be winning. You won't have that spark.

Because while you are wishing things were easier, these teams were working hard, getting smarter, building their people, their culture and their team. And winning.

Grand Final Day: Vincent and Brett holding the Champions trophy with Premier's medals and pennant

ABOUT THE AUTHOR

Brett Odgers runs a business coaching practice in his home town of Sydney, Australia. He has spent many years running creative businesses including photographic studios, film production companies, graphic design studios and even an advertising agency.

Brett is passionate about helping people achieve mastery in their lives and especially their business, because it creates abundance around him and makes the world a place that is a delight to live in. He continues his commitment to coaching at his local soccer club, having guided many teams to fun and success. He is currently volunteering as the director of coaching at his local club and is sharing this knowledge with many, many other teams.

Brett also produces online learning tools and is available for keynote speeches and workshops both in Australia and internationally. If you would like to talk to Brett about how you can create a winning team contact him at business@brettodgers.com and book in a free 10 min consultation. To find out more go to www.playingabovetheline.com

Access the online coaching program at www.playingabovetheline.com/online-coaching